I0171688

'ULU

MŪ HAWAIIAN SPINAL TECHNOLOGY: A GUIDEBOOK

KE'ONI HANALEI

DISCLAIMER:

The information in this manual is offered to supplement, not replace, proper physical training. Like any practice involving speed, movement, breath, balance, and environmental factors, this practice poses some inherent risk. The authors and publisher advise readers to take full responsibility for their safety and know their limits. Before practicing the skills outlined in this manual, be sure that your presence and temperament is well maintained, and do not take risks beyond your level of experience, aptitude, training, and comfort level. This guidebook is offered to activate your own inherent memory of humankind's profound agency. You are invited to consent yourself into your own leadership of skill and aptitude. This guidebook is not intended as a substitute for the medical advice of physicians. The reader should regularly consult a physician and/or homeopathic professional in matters relating to their health, particularly with respect to any symptoms that may require diagnosis or medical attention.

'ULU: Mū-Hawaiian Spinal Technology — A Guidebook

Copyright © 2025 by POHALA Botanicals LLC. All rights reserved.

No part of this publication may be reproduced, stored in a retrieval system, or transmitted in any form or by any means — electronic, mechanical, photocopying, recording, or otherwise — without prior written permission of the publisher, except in the case of brief quotations used in reviews or scholarly articles.

Edited by Marni Suu Alohilohi Reynolds

Book designed by Sam Aaron Creative (www.samaaroncreative.com)

TABLE OF CONTENTS

PREFACE

THE GREAT MATERIALIZATION

Before we begin the process of spiritualizing, we must first materialize.

In today's rapidly evolving world, there exists a mad dash, even a frenzied rush, to attain spiritualization, or to achieve any of the many trending terms that describe it: transcendence, ascension, transmutation, and so forth. What many individuals quite often dismiss is the very obvious fact that we are, in fact, currently undergoing a significant process of Materialization. It is only from the successful completion of this materialization that we can then embark on the journey to spiritualize.

Many prefer to outright reject the most obvious truths about our existence — that I am indeed a form, and that this form is uniquely placed in this specific location. There is truly nothing complex about this fundamental understanding. As we challenge or overlook this basic aspect of being, we simultaneously disqualify ourselves from experiencing spiritualization. The art of 'ULU stands as a prehistoric relic that supported our archaic, organic kin, aiding them in acclimating themselves to the material world. Importantly, this grounding did not come at the "cost" of becoming trapped in matter; rather, it served to bolster our potential for completing the material experience.

In Mū, the Uli represents the oversoul and serves as "criteria," while Pana is the demiurge, functioning as "fashion." In the Hawaiian language, Pana translates as "beat" and correlates to the actual rhythm of life. In this sense, the Pana is activity whereas Uli is that which activity is birthed or instructed, from. At a moment just before the Great Combustion, Source became curious about what the energy of itself and love could express in forms that could be seen, heard, tasted, felt, and evolve through measure. This profound curiosity, ignited at the time of combustion, led to the consecration of the world of matter.

From this pivotal event, intelligent and sentient formations were distributed throughout the spaces of this grand experiment, designed to portray the translations of God and the nature of ALOHA, love. This incredible feat is one of both engineering genius and artistic expression. Given that it is composed of measures, there inevitably exists a requirement for completion. It is the assembly of all these diverse expressions that pierces through the formidable constructs of existence, for the voltage of the energy of God and ALOHA is so immense that a world of form cannot contain it. This overwhelming energy marks the true moment of spiritualization.

THE MŪ EXPERIENCE

In the year 1888, the prominent theosophist Helena Petrovna Blavatsky published her influential work titled "The Secret Doctrine," in which she outlined her theories regarding the root races of humanity. The second half of the book describes the origins of humanity through an account of "Root Races," said to date back millions of years. According to her, the first root race was "ethereal"; the second root had more physical bodies and lived in Hyperborea. The third root race, the first to be truly human, is said to have existed on the lost continent of Lemuria, and the fourth root race is said to have developed in Atlantis. Among these, she identified the Lemurians as the third root race. Blavatsky derived the name Lemuria from the writings of Philip Sclater, yet she proposed that this ancient continent also existed as a higher dimension. According to her extensive claims, the landmass known as Lemuria was ultimately destroyed due to catastrophic volcanic eruptions that led to its diminishment. She posited that this vast continent existed approximately thirty-four million years ago, covering an extensive area of the Pacific Ocean and extending into the Indian Ocean, which she referred to as the "kumari" region. Blavatsky asserted that the geographical area we recognize today as South Africa, which she calls the "horse-shoe," represented the extreme outpost, where the Lemurians were said to have developed the foundational traits that would ultimately give rise to what she designated as the Atlantean root race. Therefore, she theorized that the Atlanteans emerged from South Africa before migrating northward into Europe. [1]

In my own genealogical database, we find no mention of the name or world called Lemuria. What we do have access to, however, is the name of Mū. Given the specific geographical references, the indicated timespan, cultural contexts, and the many subtle nuances consistently linked to "Lemuria," the author confidently concludes that this entity closely aligns with what is historically recognized as Mū. Much like the claims made by Blavatsky, Mū represents a foundational expression of humanity, existing long before much of what we typically consider "humanistic" or "cultural." Viewed linearly through the lens of time, this expression extends millions of years on our planet, tracing back nearly to the point of organic conception. Mū is therefore regarded as the primary civilization from which all modern cultures have ultimately blossomed. As the old Hawaiian elders would say, "If you are human, if you carry human kōkō (DNA), then you are Mū!"

Considered by many as Hawaiian "lore," Mū is a legendary land-mass that housed the very first known civilization. Predominantly located in the vast expanse of the modern Pacific Ocean, it was a unique culture that dedicated itself entirely to absorbing and embodying love into physical form. The islands of Hawai'i are widely regarded as the remaining fragments of this once-great supercontinent. Because Love, or Aloha, qualified its very essence and foundation, anything that falls out of the pure frequency of Love/Aloha can no longer access or exist within it. In this deeper sense, Mū has never truly sunk beneath the waves; instead, it simply vanished from physical presence. As humanity gradually began to numb itself to the fullness and vibrancy of Love/Aloha, we ceased to vibrate in harmony with this singular frequency, and as a result, it eventually dissolved and evaporated. Hawai'i is what remains to remind us of this profound origin.

The art of 'ULU stands as a relic of this earliest civilization, having been meticulously preserved and carefully handed down from generation to generation. By cultivating fluency in this archaic art form, we gain a deeper glimpse into the functions and intimate experiences of our ancient ancestors. If Mū was truly a full embodiment of Love/Aloha, then it makes perfect sense that 'ULU evolved into a sacred tool designed to transfer and absorb love/aloha directly into the materials of this living world. From the successful absorption of Love/Aloha into these fundamental, and galactic, materials, we then manifest love in this expression of God, thus completing it. *Is this not the very essence of spiritualization itself?*

LOVE/ALOHA

In the culture, it goes like this: *Ka Mea Nānā I Hana*, Source, God, is the surge and very essence of Aloha, love. And, God had the very first intelligence which was this profound realization: "I not only want to be BE Aloha, I want to give and receive it as well." Empowered by this conscious consent, God separated itself from itself so that it could love itself, allowing aloha to become self-reflective. We can sense this moment as the very genesis of Free Will. Aloha, or love, may very well be the original lineage and lasting legacy of our entire universe.

Over time, we have translated this powerful energy into the most exquisite ways and forms. However, regardless of how deeply or rationally we try to understand aloha, it will always remain somewhat elusive and mysterious to us. Perhaps this elusiveness acts as a safeguard, ensuring that aloha can never be controlled or constrained. Maybe our Mū kin understood that simply enjoying the experience of aloha is both sufficient and fulfilling, and if there is any definitive relationship we share with it, it is one of profound awe. The author will not attempt to rigidly define Aloha in this book, but will instead present it as a deeply guiding and inspiring force — one that has promoted our evolution and to which we all inherently belong.

HO'OMAKA'ANA (ORIGINS)

4 billion years ago, something truly monumental and transformative occurred in the form and shape of the magnetic field of Earth, setting the stage for the development of life as we know it.[2] The ancient name for our planet is Kī, which holds profound significance. When analyzed through reverse speak, the name Kī is rendered as ~ ik-e, which translates to "to feel." This represents the essential sensory experience of both material and organic elements, all founded on the rough and rocky scaffolding that constitutes our planet.

In the Mū doctrines, it is stated that a watery energy preceded the emergence of organic life. This elemental watery energy, referred to as the Mea Ne'e (translated as Plasmic beings), is believed to have designed the essential conditions for two fundamental aspects to exist: first, an atmosphere, and second, a magnetic field. These two elements are recognized as the pivotal ingredients necessary for organic life to exist, flourish, and truly thrive. Upon the successful establishment of both the atmosphere and the magnetic field, it is said that the Mea Ne'e transformed themselves into the water that has remained steadfast on this planet ever since.

According to Mū teachings, water is far more than just a life-sustaining resource; it is regarded as our actual founders and ancestral essence. From this foundational understanding, the Mū began the arduous, yet glorious process of organic materialization. The term "organic" specifically refers to compounds characterized by carbon-carbon and carbon-hydrogen bonds, whose fundamental composite derives from the ultraviolet light of stars. The "originals," as they are remembered, are thought to have possessed a luminosity akin to a radiant sphere of light, particularly in shades of blue, with a singular objective: to fully experience and embody LOVE.

The genealogy of Love persisted for millions of years, and the light bodies of the Mū began a slow titration into the predominant carbon-based structure we experience today. The carbon protocol is not erroneous; it is part of the process of Materialization. Variation of love is truly the epitome of the Mū experience, and 'ULU is resourced as a tool to support this titration, and as a method to archive the story of our founding and to track the procession into Spiritualization.

IN THE AUTHORITY OF

The Hawaiian Islands are remarkably isolated in the vast expanse of the Pacific Ocean, which effectively kept Hawaiians separate from outside influences for thousands of years. This profound isolation has significantly aided us in preserving our unique culture, which began facing various challenges only a few hundred years ago. What I share with you about 'ULU and Mū culture is specifically tied to my family, or 'ohana, and is a reflection of our shared experiences. All families across the Hawaiian Islands connect through a common ancestry, and through the oli helu, a genealogical chant, we find a meaningful connection to our roots. Each 'ohana possesses its own unique history and customs, which I refer to as accents. For instance, as a native of the island of Maui, I am able to recognize the subtle yet distinct differences in language or cultural references when engaging in conversation with someone from the island of Kaua'i, even if we are discussing the same deity or notable place. This variation becomes even more evident in our native language, 'ōlelo Hawai'i, where different family lines have their own distinctive accents that reflect their identities. I aim to share my perspective through the rich heritage of Wīwī Hoe Wa'a, Kamake'e, Hao, Lonohiwa, and our esteemed founder, Mahat. Understanding these various accents not only reveals the complexity and remarkable tolerance of ancient Hawaiian and Mū cultures but also suggests a society where competition was minimal, fostering an environment that allowed for both diversity and harmony with nature. This harmonious coexistence truly embodies Pono, or righteousness.

THE LINEAGE

Every Hawaiian has access to the oli helu, the genealogical chant. This chant is augmented and enriched with each new generation, adding layers of meaning and context. The names of ancestors and vital details are included to refine and ultimately strengthen an inexhaustible genetic legacy.

In a traditional Oli Helu, the names of relatives are carefully archived alongside notable qualities of that generation. These qualities may encompass actual historical events, memorable anecdotes, or specific characteristics of our relatives. These intricate details help us decipher the timeline as to become a complete archive.

For example, the Oli Helu of my line begins with a reference to a man named Mahat (Mahaka). In the chant, we utter the phrase *"mat xe Gert-gat turana,"* meaning "the time of the position of Alpha Cephai." From this detail, we have surmised that Mahat lived during the period when Alpha Cephei served as Earth's pole star, around 18,000 B.C.E. As we progress through the Helu, the succeeding generations support this timeline, confirming this documented lineage begins at 18,000 B.C.E

It is very unconventional for modern Hawaiians to openly "publish" their lineal record. This tradition of concealment is one reason why our genealogical knowledge remains largely uncorrupted, yet it is equally the same reason that it is slowly vanishing from collective memory.

In revealing the following names and details, I am not intending to exploit my people's heritage. Rather, this is a sincere effort and act of perseverance aimed at preservation.

The stories of my line must gain relevance in today's world.

I, as the relative with the kino (body) and leo (voice), now step forward to become the modern ambassador tasked with catapulting 20,000 years of history and tradition into the global database that is integral to the reconciliation of the fulfillment and completion of our Human Event.

PREFACE

Ke'oni Hanalei
- **Father:** Johnny Charles Baldwin *(Hawai'i)*
  - **Mother:** Gene Isabelle Mason *(British Columbia)*
    - **Mother:** Elizabeth Gillis *(Scotland)*
    - **Father:** Charlie Mason *(Scotland)*
  - **Father:** Bryan Wilfred Baldwin *(Colorado, USA)*
- **Mother:** Georgette Ka'apo'okalani *(Hawai'i)*
  - **Mother:** Margie Kau'ikeonalani Kaipo
    - **Mother:** Agnes Chang Kaluna
      - **Mother:** Julia Kawahine Kaikuwale
      - **Father:** Keokolo Kaluna
        - **Mother:** Kapehe Kuali'i
          - **Mother:** Kaila'a Kahaulua
            - **Mother:** Kamaka Ka'ua'ua
            - **Father:** Kamake'e Kuhaulua
          - **Father:** Kunukau Kuali'i
        - **Father:** Makaūla Kaluna
    - **Father:** James Kaipo
      - **Mother:** Haili Laepu
      - **Father:** Pai ela Kaipo
  - **Father:** George Elia Akina
    - **Father:** Frank Auhana Akina
      - **Father:** Auhana Boniface Akina
        - **Mother:** Lucy Luka Kalua'u
        - **Father:** Ah Sing Ah Chong Akina
      - **Mother:** Hanna Burns Pae *(O'ahu)*
        - **Mother:** Mary Makanui
        - **Father:** Joseph Keao Pae
          - **Mother:** Kaluaihaina Ahikanana
          - **Father:** Pae
    - **Mother:** Rebecca Ka'apo'okalani Mahi'ai
      - **Father:** George Mahi'ai
      - **Mother:** Naho'opi'i Kamakakahukilani Lonohiwa Kaula
        - **Father:** Maihenui Lonohiwa
        - **Mother:** Hattie Moikeahililinoe Keahienaena
          - **Father:** Kanuiokalani Keahienaena
          - **Mother:** Wiwi Hoewa'a
            - **Mother:** Wiwiokaluahine
            - **Father:** Keahiauwilamoku *(Moloka'i)*
            - **+ 103 Generations**

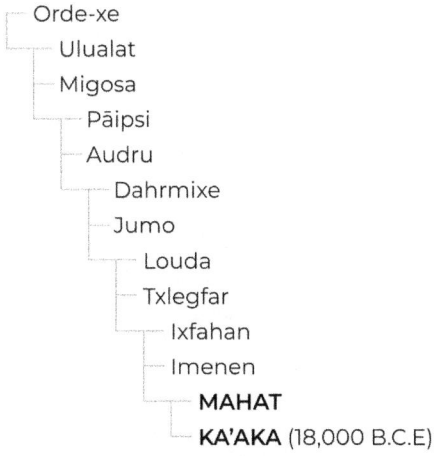

Orde-xe
Ulualat
Migosa
Pāipsi
Audru
Dahrmixe
Jumo
Louda
Txlegfar
Ixfahan
Imenen
MAHAT
KA'AKA (18,000 B.C.E)

THE MŪ DOCTRINES

The data that is held within the oli helu, alongside the intricate practice of reading the spinal cord, are considered to be legitimate doctrines of Mū. Throughout the course of this book, I will reference and draw upon information that has been meticulously retrieved from these valuable doctrines. The act of reading and comprehending the spinal cord is not just important, but paramount in preserving and understanding the foundational doctrines of Mū, just as much as its retrieval is essential. The captivating art of 'ULU is accessible to anyone who is willing and consents to embark on the journey of investigating and negotiating your own unique doctrines of Mū. Furthermore, it is worth noting that the author of this book represents an authority in this field, but not the singular or ultimate authority on the subject matter. As you cultivate your fluency and skill in the practice of 'ULU, you will inevitably begin to experience various methods of disclosure that can manifest in multiple forms.

Disclosure can feel, or seem, both literal and practical in many ways, such as through the process of remembering certain things, including symbols, names, dates, and more. These memories will begin to flood your sphere of awareness, creating a rich tapestry of understanding. You may also begin to experience sensory disclosures—things like smells, tastes, sensations, and sounds—that may lack a clear point of reference; in these moments, you will find yourself becoming that which translates these experiences into relatable and meaningful expressions. This process can at times seem vast and overwhelming, yet it is important to acknowledge and appreciate the inherent simplicity within it all. Memory often becomes overwhelming only when one feels the need to keep track of the untruths or lies that may cloud one's perception. In contrast, truth presents itself as clear patterns that can be tracked and understood easily. There is no strenuous effort involved in maintaining or cataloging these truths.

Additionally, disclosure can also manifest in what is described as "light language"—a form of communication that may initially appear strange, frightening, or even possessive to some, but only because its existence in this reality is only possible at the precise moment you allow it to enter your consciousness. In this space, I encourage you to allow it all to assemble, inviting you to be as much an observer of the unfolding process as you are an interactive participant in it. As the archives of knowledge begin to strum themselves up and down along the spinal cord, each passage you encounter is an opportunity for refinement, leading up to the apex of the sacred seven cervical vertebrae. This apex will ultimately offer you an entirely revised lens through which to see, free of the exhaustion that is often produced by the performances induced by amnesia. In the fluency of the artistry of 'ULU, you will be compelled to excel.

CHAPTER 1
WHAT IS ʻULU?

To fully understand what exactly is meant by ʻULU, we take the time to carefully deconstruct the name, ʻULU. The word has remained uncorrupted in the rich oral traditions of the Hawaiian and Mū culture, sustaining its composition as the four-lettered word ʻ - U - L - U for an impressive span of at least 20,000 years. The apostrophe mark, known as the okina, serves as a glottal stop, and when it appears as the first letter in a word, it can often suggest that the meaning of the word is informed by a sense of belonging and/or the act of establishing. This nuance is particularly important to consider regarding the art of ʻULU, in that before the word is actually spoken aloud, it must first be firmly established in context. The term ULU encompasses a multitude of meanings in both ancient Hawaiian (Mū) and modern Hawaiian language, so for our discussion, let's focus on its poetic reference, which is most accurately aligned with its proper meaning in the specific context of the art form of ʻULU.

"To enter and to inspire."

"To become occupied by a phenomenal force."

These words form the poetic translation of the term 'ULU.

———

With the glottal stop that precedes the U, L, and U sounds, we can deeply feel this as a powerful opening and an invitation, allowing us to land gracefully in order for the word to truly inhabit our existence. What this word will inhabit is YOU. It is also me. It encompasses us collectively. The organic humans, shaped thoughtfully by our plasmic ancestors, the Mea Ne'e, find their connection in the word 'ULU.

Hence, it leads us to become occupied by a phenomenal force that transcends our immediate reality.

As previously mentioned, upon Materialization, the essence that is often described as the "light body" or "light being" took up residence within the organic human form. This profound process can sometimes be traumatic, as the physical matter may serve as a limitation for the otherwise volatile and dynamic nature of quantum energy that is characteristic of the Light Body. Through the use of curated and purposeful breathing and movement techniques—each of which is centered around the spinal cord—we can support the consolidation and acclimation of the architecture and construct of our physical being. The library of these unique breathing and movement techniques consists of over 12,000 distinct practices, each of which has specific names that reveal their intended purpose and functionality. We will explore more in-depth details regarding these specific breathing and movement techniques as we progress through this book.

'ULU is initially an art form that supports the acclimation process into the physical body, as well as the intricate protocols of Materialization.

Contrary to popular belief, this understanding does not confine us solely to the realm of matter, nor does it isolate our vast potential of light; rather, it provides a vital hub through which the light can effectively assemble and organize. In this transformative state, we become literal circuitry, similar to that found in our nervous system and within the intricate canals of our blood-carrying veins and vessels that internally circumnavigate to uphold the elegant design of the sphere within. This internal circum-hydraulic system is what maintains our physical connectivity to the alpha/omega, symbolizing the uninterrupted sphere of existence. The art of 'ULU serves to remind our physical selves to behave as an assembly for the energetics of an immersive, spatial experience with the individual organic human serving as its core hub, adeptly pulling energy into a central point, akin to a refined process of organization and reconciliation. The data we experience is filtered through our internal physical structure and then reversed outward as a vibrant expression. We can readily see and feel how this act, in its essence, behaves in a circular manner, continuously repeating the cycle of energy and transformation.

With the support of 'ULU, the carbon-crystalline body could withstand the intensity and complexity of data and information that becomes signals for integration, expression, and evolution.

We can also deconstruct the oldest known mention of 'ULU, circa 18,000 B.C.:

"O ka 'umat ka 'ulu e hana ai xe ia mea, topuni, uila, e hoahu ahn a i mea, ma kahi oht-tze ulu, lilo ka ku i vahona. ohi, ohi, pa'an a veha, he hanu ia e uhane oht-tze 'ulu"

The spirit is the 'ulu that makes it the matter, encircles, vortex, accumulating a material are we, at the place of the 'ulu, the spine becomes the archive. Collect, collect, it is dense and it is hot, it is a breath that then the 'ulu spiritualizes fully.

This prose, from a cornerstone Mū prayer, describes the process of materialization and the establishment of the human being. We acknowledge this verse as recognition of birth.

"The spirit is the 'ULU that makes it the matter."

Spirit must pass through the art of 'ULU in order for proper materialization. Perhaps this is important as it describes the process of materialization free of amnesia. The spirit must pass through the art of 'ULU as to prevent amnesia.

The use of the word "mea" denotes "matter" and in addition to it suggesting intelligent matter (mea can also mean "being") it would also describe something as important/prevalent" ~ that makes it MATTER" meaning, there is attention, focus, and care in the materialization, because amnesia is not present, it literally matters.

"Encircle, vortex, accumulating a material are we, at the place of the 'ULU."

It seems to be referencing accumulation, assembly. The energetic vortex is consolidating in order to materialize. The materialization is a composition where the energies interact to propose, and then enforce, actual form. 'ULU is also synonymous with the spinal cord, and this could suggest that the ultimate convergence point is in the spine itself — the pillar, the Jed, hence "at the place of the 'ULU"

"The spine becomes the archive. Collect, collect, it is dense and it is hot."

The mention of density is clearly a reference to materialization. The reference to the spine as the archive supports the previous idea that the spine is the convergence point of the energetics coming into a central space for composition. The mention of heat is the first indication of sensation, which could be symbolic of coming into the sensation of materialization.

"It is a breath that then the 'ULU spiritualizes fully."

The reference to breath can suggest respiration, or the inhale/exhale, give-take. This is important in that it symbolizes the interactive nature of a material world. Once there is proper internal materialization, the light body is "visible" to begin to engage with other materials. Breath can also be literal, as in we take our first breath, which indicates our presence in the material world. The word used for breath, Hanu, in the old dialect, also means "other people" and "to race about," which is symbolic of acknowledging "other" materials, and "to race about" a recognition of space and time. That spiritualizes fully — it is the experience of breathing, recognizing other materials, and encompassing space and time, that allows for spiritualization.

As the Light Being became immersed and enmeshed into Matter, this rapid consolidation known as form is Materialization.

Upon the Materialization, the Ka-Naka, "quivering," the art known as 'ULU became the primary tool to assist the materials, such as Man, to acclimate itself into form. From the consolidation of the Light into the Form, we are then to Spiritualize to return to the Light. This accomplishes a full circumnavigation of the Human Event, the Earth Event, and the Event of the Material.

Depicted in the archaic prayer is the focus on the spinal cord, the Iwi Kuamo'o. Believed to be the human akasha.

Here, cosmic knowledge and memory are safeguarded. In our fluency of 'ULU, and the limber and lubricated spinal cord, we experienced simple access, and also grand disclosures that emanate from our auric field. This is why some of the ancient ancestors were known as A'a 'Ena (the shining ones).

As we breathe our spinal cord, we become breathed with the cosmos, and true affluence, of primary flow, is restored. Because there is no differential between the organic human and the cosmic flow, we begin to behave like plasma, our most fundamental property. The phrase "become breathed" is just another way to describe behaving as plasma.

From the Mū doctrines, we inherit over 12,000 movement and breathing designs that assist in this acclimation into material. Some are focused on the lower chamber of the vertebrae, the feminine domain. Others act as heart activators, centered in the thoracic vertebrae, empower and vitalize the internal masculine. And some are purely altering, in a state of trance, that reconfigure the brain glands and masses, to exult the cervical vertebrae, the androgynous self.

The ultimate objective of 'ULU, beyond access to the Akasha, is to SPIRITUALIZE. The maximum consolidation of the animate creates a cosmic pressure that, in turn, behaves as a Black Hole. Without offering too much detail, this is truly a simple translation of transfiguration and transcendence.

CHAPTER 2
THE SCIENCE OF 'ULU

The architecture of the human spine is commonly composed of 33 individual vertebrae, from the coccyx to the atlas. These 33 vertebrae are categorized in three unique chambers: the 'Unihipili (coccyx, sacral lumbar), the 'Uhane (thoracic), and the 'Aumākua (cervical).

The spine behaves much like a pillar in the central proximity of the body, informing the body like an antenna. Each vertebra holds specific codes that correlate to human consciousness. The compilation of all these 33 codes achieves what can be known as the holistic self. It is the accomplishment of the holistic self that qualifies the Hala, transfiguration.

The actual design of these chambers reveals poetic and practical references to the function of these codes. For example, the lumbar complex supports the weight of the human body, which exquisitely relates to the 5 vertebrae of the lumbar, correlating as being held, or carried, through life. We'll notice how the actual design and the poetry overlap.

We'll examine these relations as we explore these vertebral chambers further along in this guidebook.

The coccyx, sacral, and lumbar comprise the foundational chamber of the 'Unihpili. The 'Unihipili is our feminine quality. Therefore, the 14 vertebrae that comprise the 'Unihipili are the inherent codes of the internal feminine energetics. Fluency and flexibility, of these 14, determine the establishment of the feminine. As each of the 14 is properly invigorated, they begin to strum in unison, providing the proper volume that propels into the thoracic vertebrae, the 'Uhane, internal masculine

The 12 thoracic vertebrae are the 12 actions of the inherent masculine. Proper fluency of this column determines the actual infrastructure of our lives. Feel the internal masculine, as the thoracic, as the engineer, and as the artist. The 12 vertebrae are individual tools to which the internal masculine can create infrastructure. Not only do these 12 codes behave as tools, but also 12 memories of exquisite design. You'll notice that the thoracic is supported by the lumbar. This already reveals the dynamic nature of a masculine supported by the foundational feminine (earth mother). There are unique architectural qualities pertaining to the thoracic that expose the nature of the internal masculine, and how the natural masculine prefers to, and must, function. When the 'Uhane, as central pillar, maintains integrity (literally), we surmount the exalted 7 of the cervical, 'aumākua.

7 codes, 7 stages of the exalted self, are the cervical vertebrae, 'Aumākua. Just as in the lower vertebrae of 'Uhane and 'Unihipili, the actual design of the climactic complex of cervical details symbolic qualities that correlate to the codes preserved therein. For example, the cervical has three tunnels that accommodate

vessels, arteries, and nerves. This is unique to the cervical as 'Uhane and 'Unihipili only have one, the predominant Spinal Canal. In addition to the spinal Canal, 'Aumākua has two more canals located on either side of the vertebra. These additional canals are called Transverse Forman and may symbolize the cervical as a tributary where a grand convergence and dispersion happen. We'll offer more insight on this unique accessory.

According to the nuanced understanding of human physiology of the ancient civilization of Mū, the very first bone to make its appearance en utero is the hyoid bone. Located strategically just below the mandible, this U-shaped skeletal structure is unique in that it is not directly connected to any other bone, existing in a state of total suspension. The actual function of the hyoid relates significantly to the tongue, which subsequently influences critical abilities such as speaking and swallowing, thereby greatly enhancing the essential functions of both eating and language. The Hyoid informs the creation of every individual vertebra of the spine, beginning with the Atlas, the first cervical vertebra known as C1, and extending all the way down to the coccyx, which is commonly referred to as the tailbone.

During fetal development, the rough scaffolding represents our very spine, and everything—every aspect of our being—becomes informed by this foundational structure, directed toward full materialization. This important notion must be taken into account as we delve deeper into the scientific and spiritual significance associated with the spinal cord and its unique role as akasha.

The cerebrospinal fluid, which is referred to as Leke in the old dialect, behaves like a natural lubricant that not only maintains flexibility by accommodating the suspension of the spinal complex but also applies a subtle yet effective pressure onto each vertebra. This pressure acts like an ignition source that sustains a voltage, which, when shared across all 33 vertebrae, runs rhythmically up and down the spinal column, flowing into the brain masses and glands, much like a force of oscillating circuitry. This internal force field not only manifests within but also extends outward to the exterior of the physical body, curating an actual atmosphere that some refer to as the aura.

———

THE WAT-EHT

Wat-Eht is a very old word. This word shows up in chants and prayers dated 18,000 B.C. The singular word "Wat" is translated as Alpha. Interestingly, "watt" is used to describe the unit of power that measures the distribution and use of energy. The Wat, alpha, is the fine pin to which all things scatter from. It is the informant. Eht, as singular, translates as Omega. It is compelling to note that EHT, Event Horizon Telescope, behaves as a network that captures the location of Black Holes. A black hole is the supreme, and dramatic, climax of the Omega, the definitive consolidation and assembly. It is the Eht where that which has been scattered now becomes gathered.

Alpha-Omega as experienced in the bio-psychic technology of the oscillatory spinal complex.

Before we apply care to the actual energetic oscillation of the spinal cord, let's address the necessary components that provide that qualify it.

First, a journey into specific brain glands and masses. As described previously, the cervical complex, 'Aumākua, includes brain masses and glands. The Transverse Foreman, the tunnels that run on either side of the 7 cervical vertebrae, accommodate the actual wiring of the brain. As the wiring runs through them, they become enmeshed with that specific spinal complex — the Transverse Foramen is unique to only the cervical, as was already mentioned.

With this awareness, we can imagine the brain as the hub of the actual circuitry of the spinal cord. This is supported by the section of the cerebrospinal fluid, created in the brain's ventricles, which greatly supports and fashions the actual spinal cord.

Now, let's feel the hub of the brain as a kind of antenna that is receiving and transmitting information in and out of the physical body. The actual composition of the physical structure of the brain relays a kind of compatibility of the unseen energetics to locate and then infuse itself within the physical body. This is a unique type of bio-psychic-spirit channeling.

The brain masses, under such immense stimulation, detoxifies itself by secreting fluids which, as a result, carry information of that channeling. When the secretions mix with the cerebrospinal fluid, it then drips down the spinal cord, in total, from C1/Atlas to the coccyx, and then shoots back up.

As mentioned previously, the fluids, when applied to the vertebra, behave as a subtle ignition that, when paired with the data of the fluid, is a kind of nutrient that we really don't have a word for in modern context, but has been called Kulu Kurut in the Paleolithic times.

This very specific combination is the actual key to Akasha.

THE PINEAL AND PITUITARY

Two very specific glands are essential in the composition of the Kulu Kurut.

First, we have the cone-shaped gland Pineal, a storehouse of masculine energy. The primary function of the Pineal Gland is the secretion of Melatonin. Melatonin greatly determines our very rhythm. Rhythm, as a verb, is the masculine component. In proper stimulation, resulting in detox, the Pineal will secrete a clear, golden substance likened to honey. That to which it secretes is the data that is being detoxed from it.

Secondly, and just as important, we have the Pituitary, the inherent feminine gland. Located at the base of the brain, the Pituitary gland is foundational as an informant of fertility (in men and women), cell replication, and hormones that attune us to our feelings and emotions. The pituitary secretes a milky substance, and as mentioned prior, stores the very information that is being detoxed from it.

These two separate secretions must meet and negotiate a merging. This is done in the mass known as the Claustrum. Let's acknowledge this thin layer of grey matter as the mediator of the unifying fluids. It is important to note that memory is the primary function of the claustrum. We sense actual memory as the organization of the collision of the polarizing landscape of feminine and masculine.

Once combined, the pineal secretion (honey) and the Pituitary (milk) are augmented to the cerebrospinal fluid, creating a trinity, and a true human, biological, elixir. Some have noted this as the human essential oil.

From the Claustrum, by way of proper "strumming," this elixir will then accomplish its tour of every human vertebra. The sacred drip will complete its descent at the coccyx, and with maintained oscillation, will be shot back up to salve the spine a second time. As the resurrection occurs, the elixir, the "nutrient" of the Kulu Kurut, meets itself back to the brain glands and masses. This time, they are not segregated but rather maintained in unison as they meet the brain once again.

It's important to note that as the elixir smears each vertebra, it also begins to collect unique information of each to which it carries to the brain. In a sense, the kulu kurut is transferring those unique codes to become exalted in the brain.

As it is applied to the brain, it is refined and sent back down. Once it reaches the coccyx, again, it will be shot back up. This repeats itself indefinitely, and the speed will also become amplified to where the measurement of the motion down to up, up to down, becomes so rapid it cannot be measured; it becomes one fantastic light that is indistinguishable from anything else. This is the Wat-eht, the Alpha/Omega moment.

––––––

PIEZOELECTRICITY AND WAT-EHT

If there is an objective of 'Ulu, it would be the Wat-eht. Let's dive deeper into the actual science of the Wat-Eht, specifically relating to Piezoelectricity.

The term Piezoelectricity is derived from the Greek word *piezein*, which translates as "to press." Within the intricate systems of the human body, there exists a fascinating phenomenon: when there is an application or friction of internal objects, a pressure is generated that leads to the creation of electricity. Remarkably, there is about 0.07 volts of electricity present in each cell of the human body, which means that within our cellular makeup, there lies immense potential for generating significant amounts of electricity. Moreover, there is also an electrical charge that is produced when pressure is applied "pre-internal" or a force that informs the actual structure of the physical body. This can be experienced as a third stage of electrical generation—the first stage being the resting electricity, akin to that which resides within the cells themselves. The second stage involves the amplification of this resting electricity, characterized by an increase in intensity, while the third stage manifests as a foreign voltage that emerges from within the body without having a prior residence. This intriguing phenomenon can be likened to portals, wormholes, or akasha-gates that become strangely accessible. It is perhaps less commonly known that the pineal and pituitary glands are encircled by microscopic crystals, forming a luminous fortress of transmitters. As oscillation travels up and down the spinal column, it accumulates magnetic pressure, which is subsequently applied to these crystals. The voltage produced in this process is referred to as piezoelectricity, creating portals through which memories enter and exit, much like a sacred shrine. An akashic harvesting occurs, and because this energy moves with oscillation, it absorbs the entirety of the spinal cord. As the measurement of this phenomenon closes in on itself, all that ultimately remains is the brilliant light of revelation, known as the Wat-eht.

In the ancient old tales, the greatest expression of purity, or purification, is metaphorically represented as being reduced to plasma. In the Mū tradition, this transformative substance is recognized and referred to as I'o. The closest reference we have to I'o, within both popular and esoteric culture, is the enigmatic concept of Fohat, or ectoplasm. This captivating substance serves as the animating force that potentially draws forth an indescribable energy from some unknown and mysterious place, and subsequently births it within our animate perspective and perception. Within the complexity of the human body, we possess a special substance, an elixir that bears a striking similarity to I'o, which is known as Kulu. Kulu is formed by the intricate combination of the sections of the pineal and pituitary glands that are united and fused within the claustrum, a central mass located in the brain. This unique combination is then released into the cerebrospinal fluid, or iwi wai, allowing it to become a vital lubricant that drips down the spinal cord, only to be shot back up. It is this essential lubricant that effectively transfers and translates the data and information emanating from the 33 vertebrae of the human spinal cord.

In the continuous oscillation of this up and down behavior, each and every impact the substance has on the brain glands generates a fascinating phenomenon known as piezoelectricity. What is ultimately accomplished, in this intriguing piezoelectric system, is the actual revelation of crucial data and information, which can be understood as cosmic disclosure.

CHAPTER 3
THE ART OF 'ULU

'ULU is truly an exquisite art form, as well as a remarkable artifact. The poetic properties of 'ULU are indeed colossal, with the intricate spinal cord serving as the sturdy scaffolding and the eminence of the chemical secretions acting as the delicate brush strokes that craft a masterpiece from unexpected and unfamiliar colors. The entirety of this remarkable work of art is what I poetically refer to as enchanted physics. Let us take a moment to acknowledge the art of 'ULU as not just a representation, but as the profound translation of the feelings we experience from its raw science, and the ways in which we give definition to those sensations. As we begin to translate the multifaceted feeling of 'ULU, we start to hear the subtle orchestration of its essence and see a design that is truly unaccustomed to basic reason and logic. This experience is akin to understanding the actual "behind the scenes" of that which is usually more visible or seemingly reasonable.

The spinal cord is prorated into three sections:

'UNIHIPILI
(coccyx, sacral, lumbar)

'UHANE
(thoracic)

'AUMĀKUA
(cervical)

———

'UNIHIPILI

'Unihipili is inherent feminine energy.

Feminine energetics is not determined solely by sex or gender; it's a vibe, and an energy that encompasses everything. Everything has a composition of feminine energy.

"Feminine" energy has been defined and described as the NOUN of all things, encompassing the essence of existence itself. The term noun refers to something that is established, belongs to, confirmed, and exists in its own right. Everything that I have just mentioned here represents the actual translation of true safety. Therefore, it is truly the energetic feminine that governs the concept of true safety. The actual symbol that represents feminine energy, particularly in the context of Mū, is the upside-down capital T. In the realm of Chinese hieroglyphics, this symbol is directly related to the idea of autonomy. Autonomy, in this context, signifies "my right to exist." Mathematically, this symbol confirms the presence of two right angles, representing stability and establishment. Here, we *innerstand* that the basic power of feminine energetics is fundamentally to affirm belonging and to certify inherent rights to be firmly established. This understanding gives a much deeper meaning to the phrase "Earth Mother." These principles are not only self-reflective; they are also recognized and accepted within the exterior conditions of our world. This indicates that inherent feminine energy can also embrace the rights, belonging, and establishment of other things and people, in addition to its own unique self. This is precisely why we often sense our feminine energy governing aspects such as diplomacy, community engagement, and even the deeply human qualities of compassion and empathy.

Within the spinal structure, the 'UNIHIPILI comprises the coccyx, sacral, and lumbar vertebrae. These three seemingly separate anatomical portions are united as the 3 within the 3, forming a cohesive whole. Altogether, they total 14 vertebrae, each of which individually holds a unique and specific code for achieving total spinal hygiene. We innerstand these 14 codes as inherently feminine, and our fluency and success in embodying these unique codes will ultimately determine our skill in moving up the spinal cord during our chemical and poetic journey toward the critical brain glands and mass. The 3 houses of the internal feminine carry the profound potential to facilitate the birth of our mature self; one that is independent, diplomatic, versatile, reliable, and keenly aware.

The presence of the inherent feminine is a true embodiment of what constitutes effective leadership. In the Hawaiian culture, we express this concept with the term ALAKA'I. A true leader possesses the wisdom to delegate responsibilities accordingly. Delegation, in this context, refers to the fair and mindful distribution of tasks and responsibilities, ensuring that everyone has an opportunity to participate meaningfully and contribute to the overall well-being of the collective whole. Contrary to misguided notions, a true leader does not engage in domination or control. This type of leader will not derive satisfaction from hoarding all the power and prestige for themselves. Instead, a leader genuinely appreciates and recognizes the diverse skills and unique properties of each individual, fostering collaboration and inclusion through effective delegation. This approach also serves to ensure that the leader is never left feeling depleted or burdened by their role. We can attribute this important skill to feminine energy, which is often and rightly associated with the essence of true community. Unfortunately, in a patriarchal society, we have often mistranslated arrogance, excessive dominance, and tyranny as authentic leadership, obscuring the true qualities that define an effective leader.

———

'UHANE

'Uhane is the inherent masculine energy.

Masculine energetics is not determined solely by sex or gender; it's a vibe, and an energy that encompasses everything. Everything has a composition of masculine energy.

"Masculine" energy is defined and described as the VERB of things, embodying the essence of action and movement. In contrast, feminine energy can be characterized as the noun, representing the static and foundational aspects of existence. While the masculine represents the dynamic activity and force driving the noun, it is the underlying vibrancy and expressive nature that signifies the intrinsic masculine force, the very essence that builds and engineers actual infrastructure around us. It is through our masculine energy that we can effectively transfer and translate the feminine realm into tangible infrastructure, allowing our dreams and fantasies to manifest as experiences within a practical, livable reality.

The feminine aspect provides an essential sense of safety, while the masculine plays a crucial role in embodying that safety; thus, this duality presents a more accurate definition of what security truly means. Elements such as food, shelter, and water exemplify the basic necessities, or priorities, that the 'Uhane diligently maintains for accessibility. One of the significant challenges lies in ensuring that these vital resources are provided in a manner that emphasizes QUALITY. Furthermore, the 'Uhane is committed to ensuring that safety and a sense of belonging are not only established but also properly protected and honored over time, ensuring their longevity. The endurance of a life characterized by quality living becomes a source of great enjoyment for the masculine as the provider.

The masculine role is qualified and measured against the thoracic vertebrae, which are located directly at the center of the spinal cord. The twelve vertebrae of the thoracic section are often seen as the twelve actions that collectively shape our existence. Each of these twelve vertebrae carries a unique code that contributes to the proper function and success of our internal engineer. When all twelve codes are applied fluently, the engineer within us matures into a sensual rhythm, transcending the potentially sterile demeanor of just an architect or a builder to become the ARTIST. The emergence of artistry is, perhaps, the greatest embodiment of the internal masculine energy, allowing for a celebration of creation in its fullest expression.

The presence of internal masculine energy can be powerfully felt as a profound sense of true heroism. In the beautiful Hawaiian language, we refer to a hero as ME'E, which signifies not just an esteemed title but a vital and essential role within our communities. A hero is someone who actively engages in producing, creating, and providing tangible and meaningful results that positively impact others. As the artist of infrastructure, that which we create in the form of livable life ultimately becomes the very evidence of our sincere endeavors. It is our inherent masculine energy that holds a deep appreciation for tangible evidence; another term associated with this significant notion is EMBODIMENT. A true hero does not simply report on their sense of belonging, nor do they merely share their dreams and fantasies; rather, they take the committed steps necessary to produce a meaningful outcome from those aspirations. This constructive process ultimately leads to a profound sense of fulfillment. Conversely, those who remain unfulfilled, often distract themselves through superficial commentary and mere reporting of their thoughts, frequently find themselves in a dispirited state of humiliation, which reflects poorly on their inherent masculine identity. This humiliated masculine energy may ultimately either revolt against itself or completely shut down. Yet, when the masculine energy courageously takes the initiative to thoughtfully design and produce the infrastructure of its dreams and fantasies, it opens the door to achieving the profound fulfillment that so many individuals passionately thirst for. It is within this pivotal moment of contentment that we can genuinely make significant progress into the stages of exaltation, represented by the cervical vertebra, known as the 'Aumākua.

ʻAUMĀKUA

The ʻAumākua is an inherent androgynous energy.

Androgynous energetics is not solely a matter of sex or gender; it's a vibe, and an energy that encompasses everything. Everything has a composition of androgynous energy.

Another term for androgynous is HOLISTIC. The energetic agency that embodies the right relationship between both feminine and masculine qualities represents the complete composition of the energetic body, which is referred to as holistic. Holistic has been defined as the concept that no single part is fully comprehensible without referencing the entirety. As we navigate through and experiment with masculine and feminine energies individually, there tends to be a tendency to play favorites. This bias is especially prevalent when we associate ourselves solely by our gender or sex. For instance, I am an anatomical male, and therefore, there is a societal expectation for me to favor and exaggerate my masculine qualities. If I prioritize my masculine side, this consequently leads to a deprivation of my inherent feminine qualities. I often emphasize that while I identify as a gender male, I am also 100% feminine, and I am equally 100% masculine. In this sense, I am energetically holistic. As I proclaim and firmly believe in this constitution, I find myself removed from favoritism, which allows me to experience the holistic essence of my being. Here, in ʻAumākua, my feminine qualities become indistinguishable from my masculine traits, and vice versa. I am accessing and resourcing those potentials simultaneously, creating a harmonious balance within myself.

As previously discussed, it is my feminine essence that uniquely establishes my identity and place in the world. I truly belong. I unequivocally possess a right to exist fully and authentically. I am an invaluable resource in my own right. From this initial and powerful proclamation, I can then confidently act upon those deeply held beliefs. The acting upon—this manifestation of intent—is the action of the masculine force. Now, I engage in the process of crafting and cultivating a tangible infrastructure of my own belonging. I deliberately design a life that reflects my true self. I am the artist of my own existence. Feel this partnership as a dynamic torsion, one that is perpetually nourished and informed by its own vibrant exchange. Having such profound access to this generative energy is what constitutes the holistic experience. In the anatomy of my being, the 'Aumākua is represented by the seven cervical vertebrae of the spinal column. These intricate spinal features begin their journey at the base of the neck, with C1 extending upward to the opening of the chamber of the skull at C7, the atlas. What is particularly unique and fascinating about the 'Aumākua is that it also encompasses the brain glands and distinct masses that play a crucial role in my overall functioning. Glands, such as the Pineal and Pituitary, would thus be considered vital members of the Cervical vertebra family. This is an essential detail to acknowledge because it suggests that the various functions and productivity of these glands and masks directly constitute the power and potential of the holistic self.

The Cervical is known as the Exulted 7, a designation that reflects its remarkable importance and function within the body. The exulted self lies herein, representing the unique capabilities of this region. The 7 cervical vertebrae behave as the most flexible segment of the spinal column and can actually fold themselves in various ways. As you bend your head forwards and backwards, you are actively flexing its potential, showcasing it as the most limber part of the entire spinal cord. In addition to the spinal canal, which is shared with the majority of the whole cord, the cervical region also features two smaller additional canals known as the transverse foramen. These smaller canals, located on opposite ends of each of the 7 vertebrae, act as a vital throughway for additional nerves and arteries to facilitate the necessary connections from the brain to the lower body. For this reason, the cervical region is particularly influential and is heavily influenced by the masses of the brain.

From C1 to C7, we actively strum the unique and intricate codes of the exulted, holistic self, engaging with each layer of our being. The fluency and deep understanding of these essential codes ultimately determine the ripeness and efficiency of the profound transfiguration that occurs as we transition from the material realm into the realm of spirit, a shift that is both significant and transformative. Historically, the actual "location" of the hub of the 'Aumākua is known to reside approximately three inches above the crown of the head, an exact point of vital energy. From this precise proximity, there exists an invisible cord that runs through the crown, gracefully descends into the head, and tethers the entire spinal cord in a remarkable defiance of gravity, thereby accomplishing the energetic buoyancy and levitation of the material self, allowing for a sense of lightness and elevation. In the accomplishment of the cervical 'aumākua, our MANA erupts powerfully from the crown and overflows, formulating a mysterious and etheric substance that gently salves and lubricates our physical form, preparing us thoroughly for the birth canal into the next transformative experience. Of course, this profound transition can only be genuinely achieved upon the fluency of the exalted 7 codes, which act as guiding principles. The exalted 7 codes require a deep fluency of the masculine 12 actions, and notably, the masculine 12 actions must be sufficiently informed by the intricate 3 within the 3 of the feminine 'Unihipili. This sacred protocol represents a vital process of Spiritualization achieved through the pathway of Materialization, creating a bridge between the physical and the spiritual realms.

———

THE 33 TONES

The human vertebrae are bestowed with the remarkable ability to produce an utterance, a distinct sound, a unique expressive code. Because of this intricate design, each of the vertebrae, amounting to a total of 33, possesses its own unique song. We remember this complex orchestration as a melodic succession gracefully moving from the coccyx to the Atlas (C1) and culminating in the brain's glands and masses. The entirety of the spinal cord emerges as a grand musical masterpiece, where each resonant tone serves as a gateway to deeper meaning; each note represents a unique rendition of the human saga that is destined for fulfillment.

As the vertebrae express itself, and subsequently translate these expressions, we recall the complete composition of our journey towards exultation. Beginning in the 'Unihipili, the Earth Mother feminine, we establish the essential assets of autonomy necessary to rise into engagement with the infrastructure, 'Uhane, of our human existence. From the artistry radiating from this duo, we are subsequently born into the exaltation of the holistic, androgynous self, 'Aumākua, revealing the final stages of our materialization.

The memory, along with the utterance, of the 33 tones is administered as a fundamental and vital bio-psychic technology that every person of Mū holds sacred. There exist cherished memories of children's games, such as Nā'ū, which encourage playful and enjoyable methods of recollection and artistry. In Nā'ū, the child takes a deep inhale and confidently utters all 33 tones in one flowing exhale. This engaging "game" of Nā'ū persists even today, but is more commonly recognized as a sport focused on determining who can maintain the longest exhale. Nā'ū is merely one example of the creative and celebratory ways through which we honor the memory and expression of the 33 tones.

Total fluency in the 33 tones and their correlating codes represents the essential prerequisite for spiritualization.

Beginning with the coccyx and skillfully progressing into the cervical vertebrae, we encounter the complete set of 33 tones, each intricately connected to the vertebrae that they support:

Coccyx

CO4 "KA" (pronounced *kah*)
CO3 "LU" (pronounced *lou*)
CO2 "KO" (pronounced *koe*)
CO1 "HA" (pronounced *ha*)

Sacrum

S5 "LI" (pronounced *lee*)
S4 "ONE" (pronounced *own*)
S3 "HI" (pronounced *hee*)
S2 "WA" (pronounced *vah*)
S1 "I" (pronounced *e*)

Lumbar

L5 "MI" (pronounced *me*)
L4 "KU" (pronounced *koo*)
L3 "MA" (pronounced *mah*)
L2 "XE" (pronounced *shay*)
L1 "G(r)A" (pronounced *gara*)

Thoracic

T12 "EX" (pronounced *etch*)

T11 "UM" (pronounced *oom*)

T10 "UN(d)" (pronounced *oond*)

T9 "JA" (pronounced *jah*)

T8 "HE(x)" (pronounced *hesh*, uttered as a sigh)

T7 "JUT" (pronounced *jooht*)

T6 "GOL" (pronounced *goal*)

T5 "AM" (pronounced *ahm*)

T4 "PA" (pronounced *pah*)

T3 "TZE" (pronounced *tzh*)

T2 "NUUT" (pronounced *nout*)

T1 "RESH" (pronounced *resh*)

Cervical

C7 "VO" (pronounced *vou*)

C6 "SHE" (pronounced *say*, uttered as a sigh)

C5 "IMA-NUT" (pronounced *e-mah-noot*)

C4 "GESTA-UT" (pronounced *gay-stah-oot*)

C3 "HEX" (pronounced *hex*)

C2 Axis "AMA" (pronounced *ah-mah*)

C1 Atlas "RA" (pronounced *rah*)

THE 33 CODES OF THE 33 TONES

Our phenomenal universe, itself, is a riddle. Therefore, everything that comprises this Universe is also a riddle. Each tone is a symbol of poetic meaning that, when translated, forms a unified composition. This composition describes the actual protocol of our path of Materialization and, upon fluency, authorizes our very Spiritualization.

First, let's take all 33 tones, combined, to form a coherent paragraph:

Ka-lu-ko-ha-li-one-hi-wa-i Mi-ku-ma-xe-ga-ex um-un-ja he-jut-gol-am-pa-tze nuut-resh-vo-she ima-nut-gesta-ut-hex-ama-ra

I then translate this text, resourcing modern dialects that are believed to be offshoots of Mū ~ Ainu, Hawaiian, Mayan, Xaad Kil, and we arrive at:

The scattering, and then gathering, as to fulfill the polarizing landscape, resulting in the expression of the Mother whom instructs the Breath and Light to produce the animated self presented as the reckless gods or the wide-opened laughter, as to determine the high potential in the convergence of the code of levitation and self-reflective Love.

What presents itself is a coherent, simplified statement of human existence. The code of such is posited confidently and soundly in the human spinal cord — in every human spinal cord. We can hold this in esteem as a foundational principle, a doctrine, of humanity's purpose and presence on this planet, in the human event. We can also match this doctrine to the three centers of the feminine (the Mother), masculine (animated self), and androgyny (code of levitation).

Furthermore, let's assess each tone individually and examine its unique code. As we familiarize ourselves with the codes that define the tone, we begin to strum the entirety of the spinal cord, resulting in a song that exists within us.

'UNIHIPILI
COCCYX, SACRUM, LUMBAR

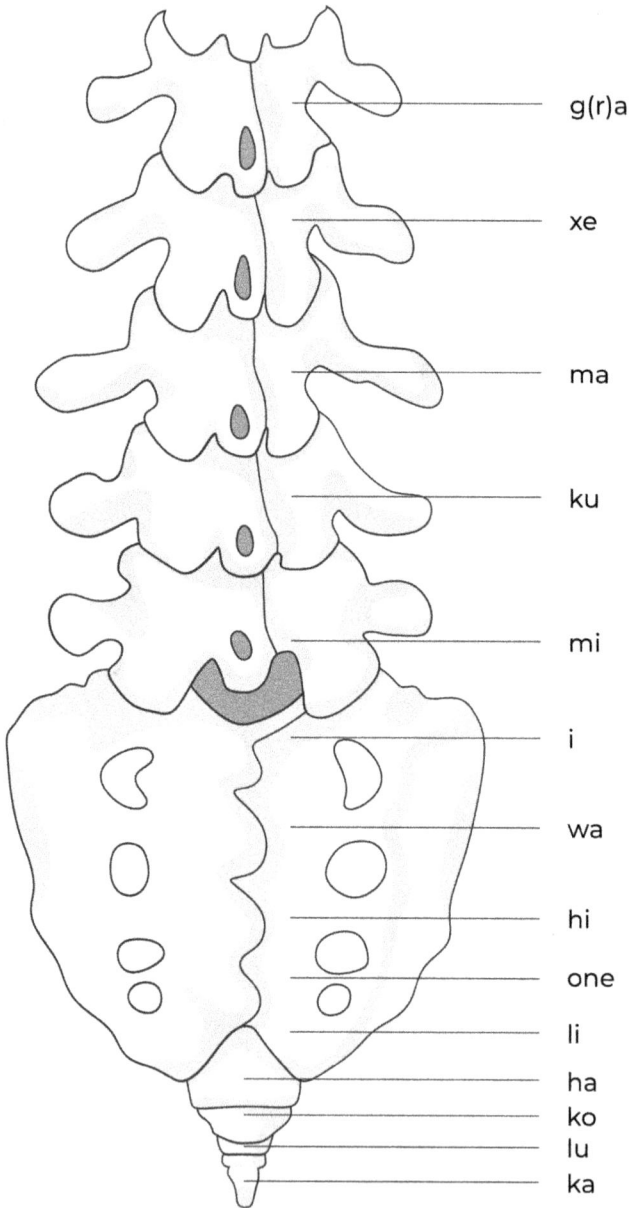

g(r)a

xe

ma

ku

mi

i

wa

hi

one

li

ha
ko
lu
ka

START HERE

Notes:

'UHANE
THORACIC

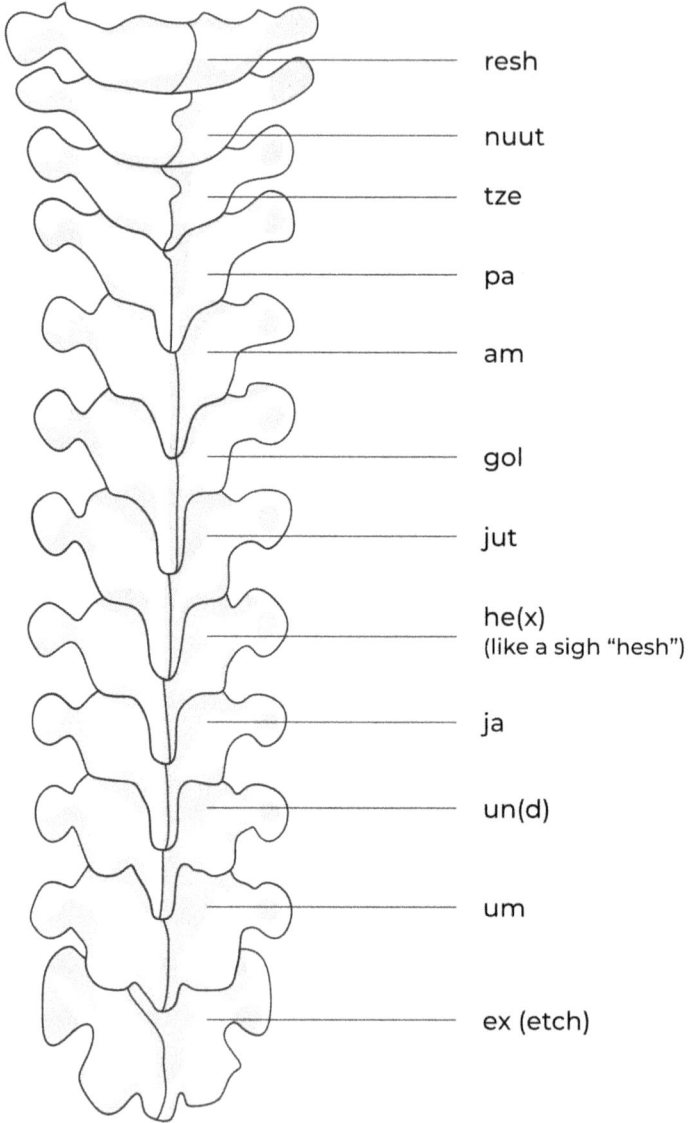

resh

nuut

tze

pa

am

gol

jut

he(x)
(like a sigh "hesh")

ja

un(d)

um

ex (etch)

Notes:

'AUMĀKUA
CERVICAL

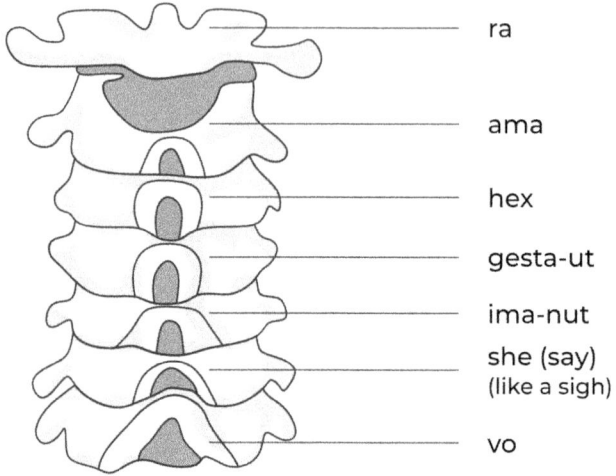

ra

ama

hex

gesta-ut

ima-nut

she (say)
(like a sigh)

vo

Notes:

CHAPTER 4
THE CODES

CHAPTER 4

COCCYX

The coccyx is shaped like an upside-down triangle.

This shape represents the strongest reference to "stability," and is commonly referenced with feminine energy.

This could suggest the coccyx codes inform and affirm neutrality, equilibrium, and balance.

The upside-down triangle points to the floor and symbolizes groundedness.

CO4
HOMEOSTASIS

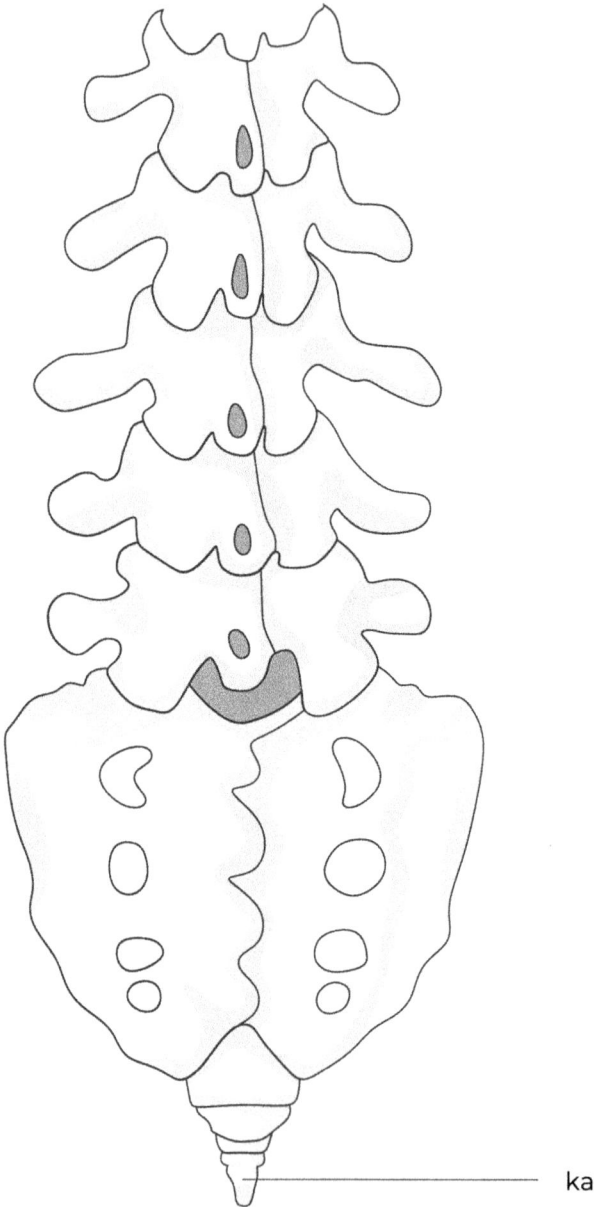

ka

CO4 — "KA"

HOMEOSTASIS

We begin in balance. Homeostasis may also be translated as equilibrium, or point zero. From the foundation of Homeostasis, everything will begin to take shape.

Clog: Amnesia, confusion

Notes:

CO3
PRESENCE

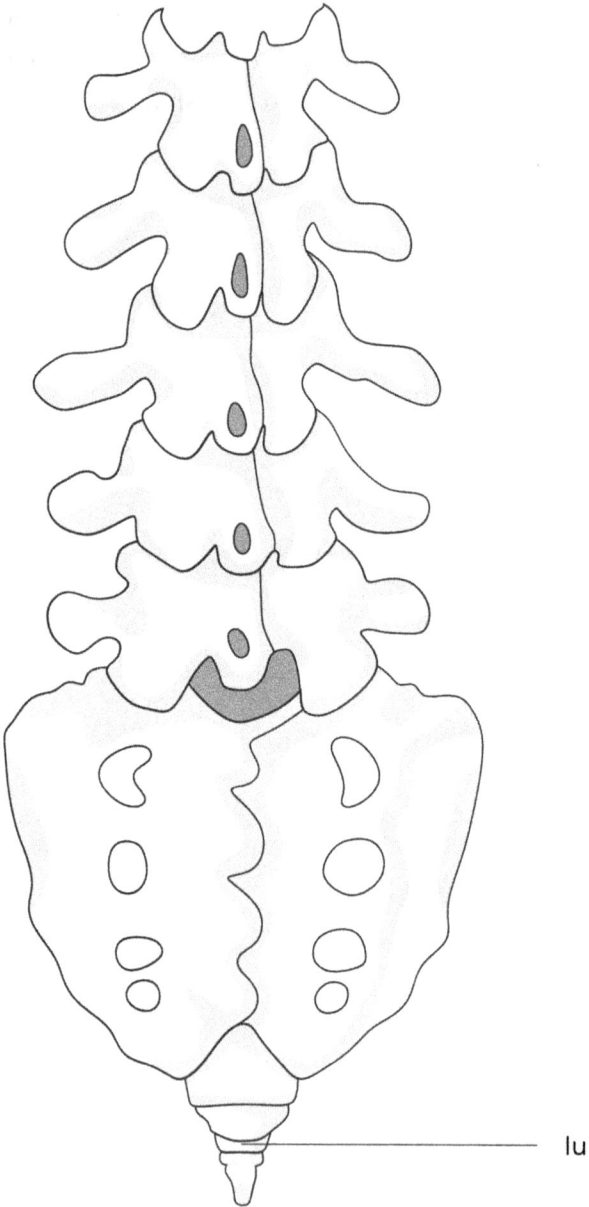

lu

CO3 — "LU"

PRESENCE

From the foundation of equilibrium, sentience is affirmed, the being is self-reflective and aware of its potential to construct itself and to acknowledge the constructs that exist outside of it. In presence, there is also the recognition that what is outside of it may also be perceived as it is; mutual reflection is possible.

Clog: Escapism, ungroundedness

Notes:

CO2
BELONGING

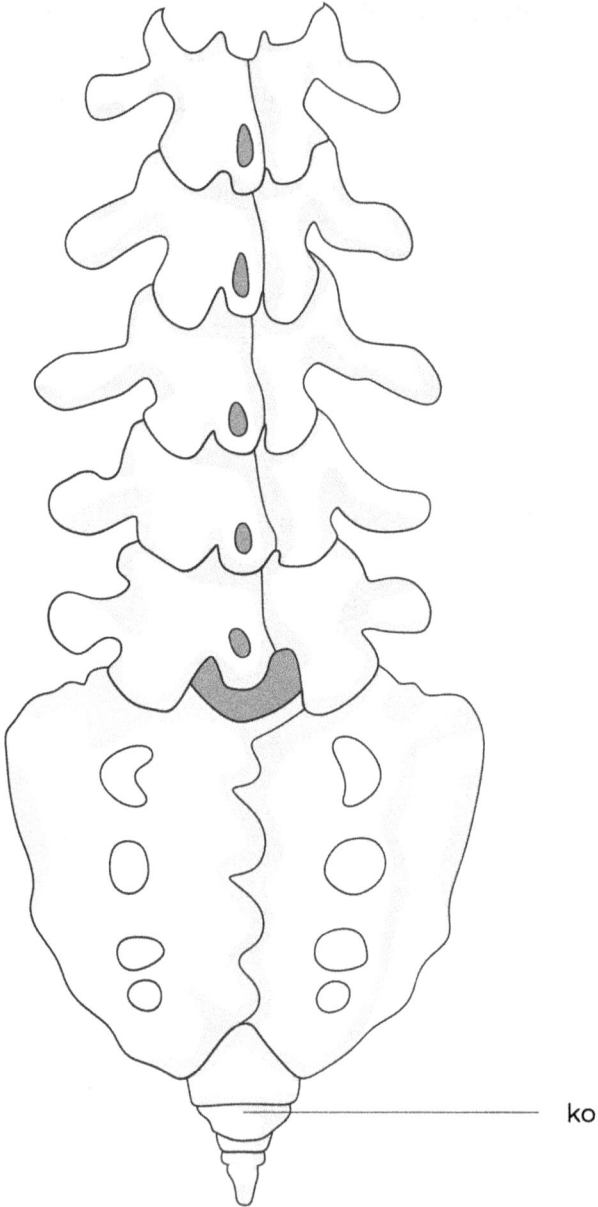

ko

CO2 — "KO"

BELONGING

I belong. You belong. We belong. The perception of self and other is confirmed, established, and belongs.

Clog: Self-dismissal

Notes:

CO1
REPLICATION

ha

CO1 — "HA"

REPLICATION

As the sentient becomes self-aware and reflectively aware, it begins to experiment with its own sentience. The awareness of belonging moves and begins to apply itself into a design, and this design becomes replicable.

Clog: Hoarding, hiding

Notes:

CHAPTER 4

SACRAL

The 5 vertebrae of the sacrum fully fuse together between 18-30, and represent coming into maturity.

For this reason, the codes of the sacrum may correlate to identity, perceptions of self, self-reliance, and gift recognition.

The sexual organs correlate to the sacrum and may relate to impulses and instinct.

S5
PSYCHIC POTENTIAL

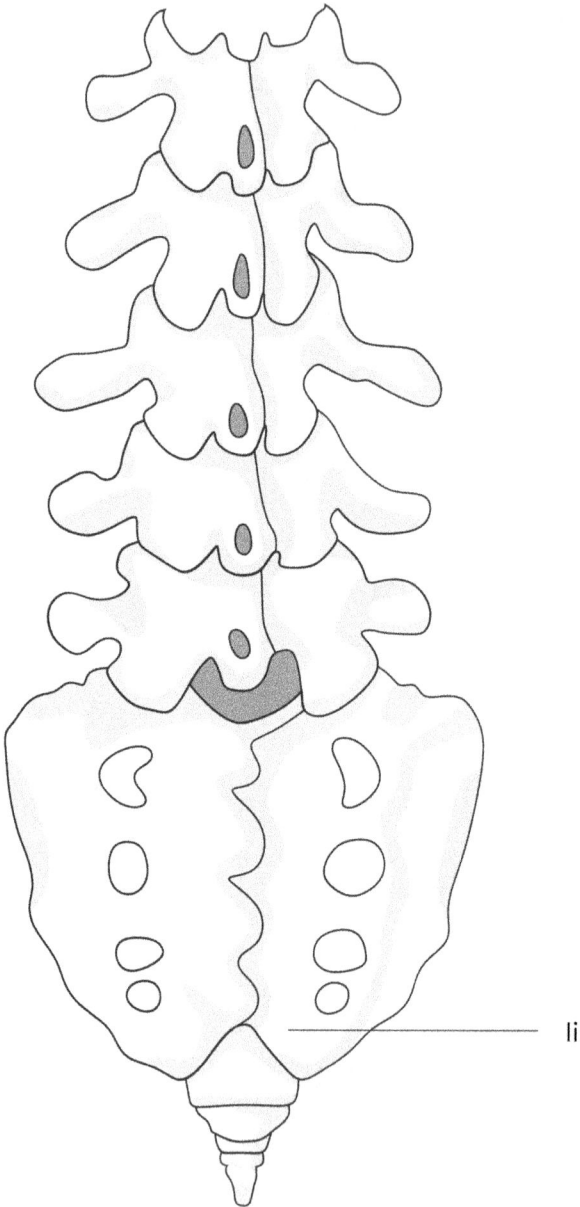

li

S5 — "LI"

PSYCHIC POTENTIAL

As the being becomes self-aware and perceptive, it achieves the skill of reading and/or sensing the quality of energy that co-exists. Psychic Potential is knowing how patterns present and function. From pattern recognition, the being can then inner-stand the grander design of things.

Clog: Mania

Notes:

S4
TRANSMITTING PORT

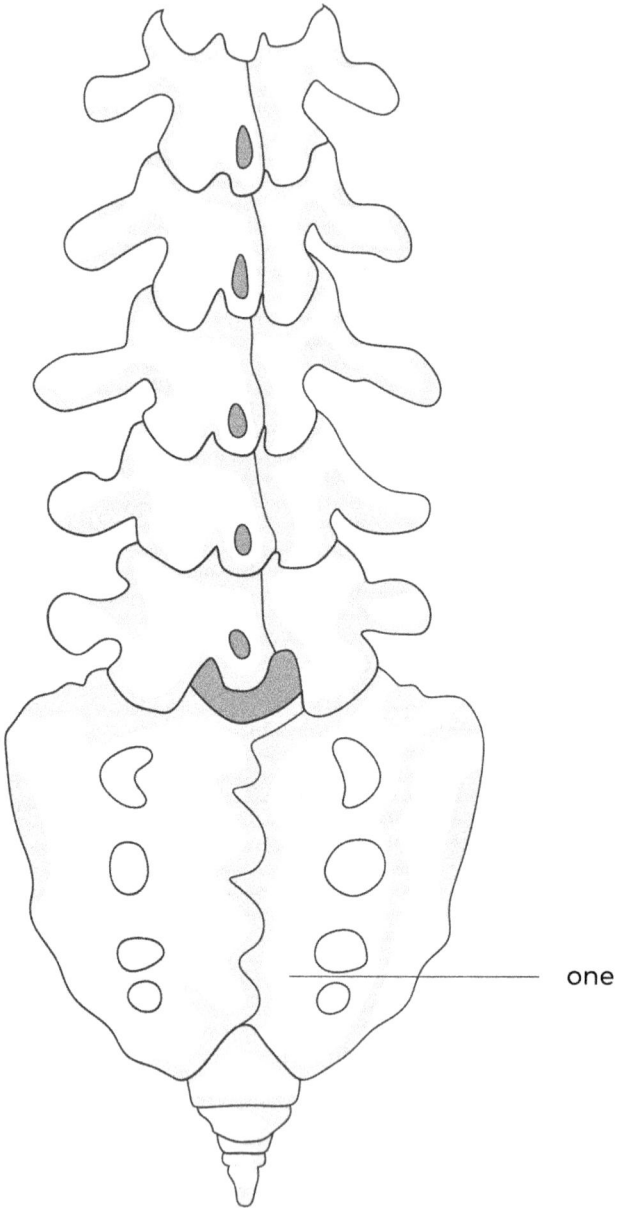

one

S4 — "ONE"

TRANSMITTING PORT

As the design presents itself, the being can now alchemize it, play with it, edit, and augment. The transmitting port functions much like an antenna. The being's reception and receptivity are determined by this skill, including the quality and clarity of it.

Clog: Social phobias

Notes:

S3
PERMEABILITY

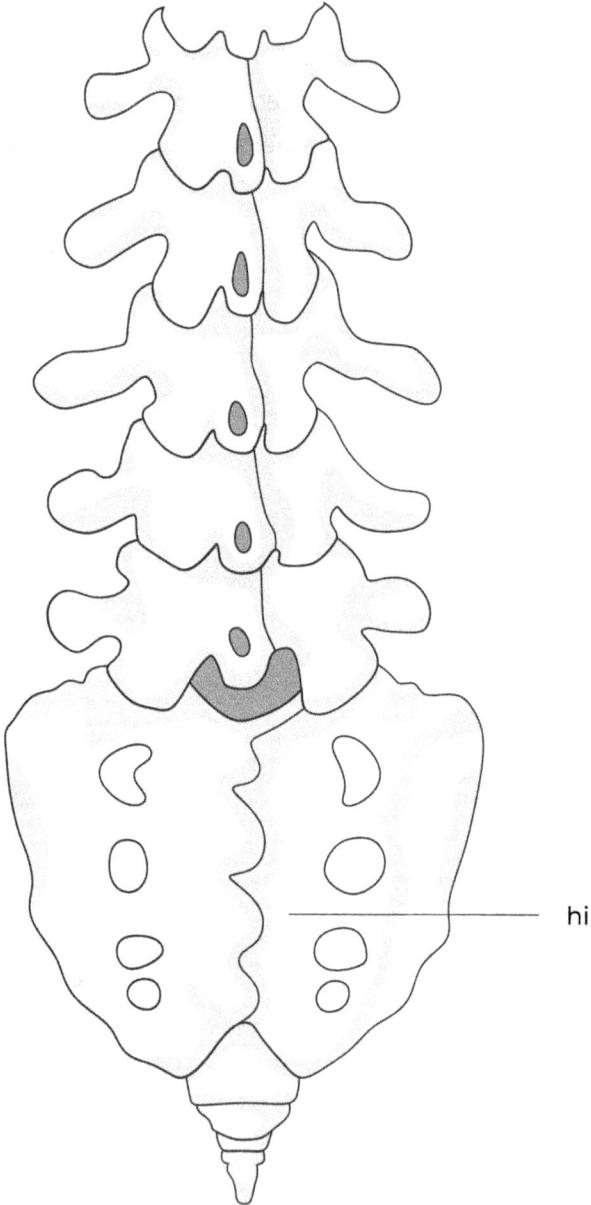

hi

S3 — "HI"

PERMEABILITY

Permeability is the liminal space that dances and allows contrast. As the design and pattern of a reality present itself, we notice the magnitude of its contrast and variation. Permeability maintains the being's skill to withstand the variation free of feeling threatened or overwhelmed by such contrast.

Clog: Control

Notes:

S2
DISCERNMENT

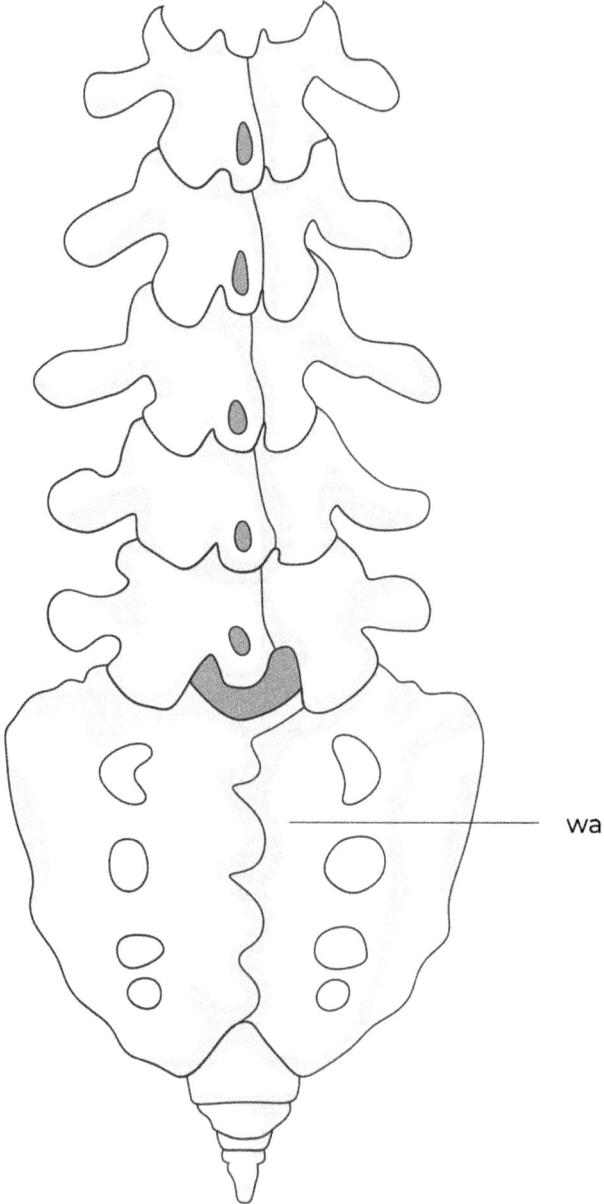

wa

S2 — "WA"

DISCERNMENT

Discernment allows for decision-making and belief-building. From the permeability of a design of variation and contrast, discernment grants *choice*. Discernment provides confirmation of what is essential, alleviating the self of excess and non-essential, or fantastical, ideology.

Clog: Overwhelm, fantasizing, unrealistic

Notes:

S1
DIPLOMACY

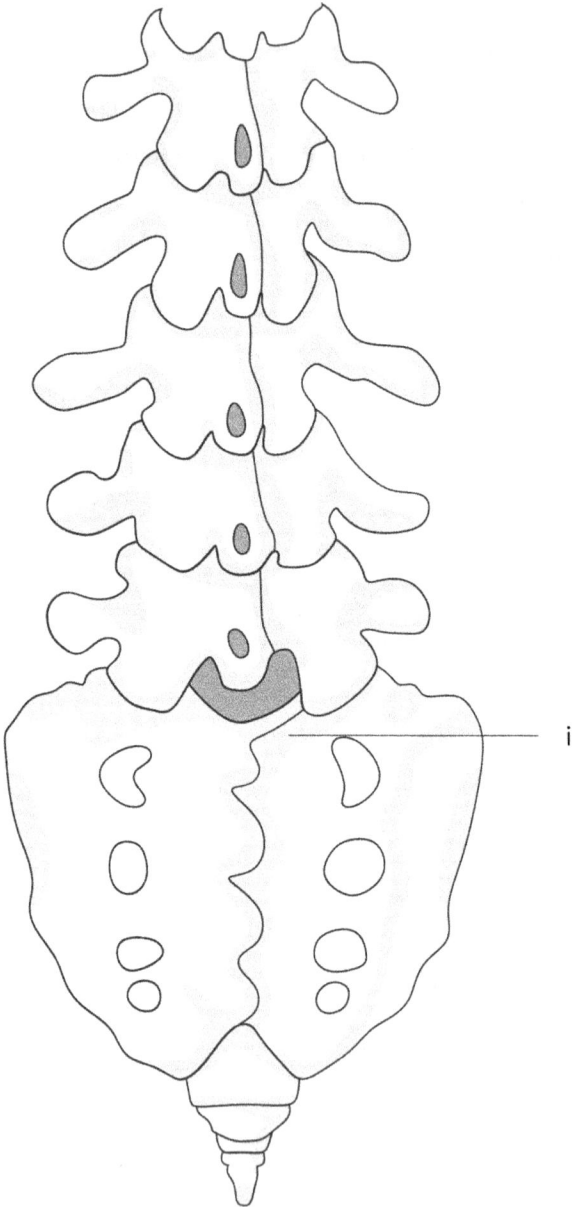

i

S1 — "I"

DIPLOMACY

From the skill of discernment, the being makes sovereign choices true to its own self-awareness and, in diplomacy, as diplomatic, allows for the variation of choices that others select. It is diplomacy that alleviates non-essential competition.

Clog: Non-essential competition, intolerance

Notes:

CHAPTER 4

LUMBAR

The lumbar carries the weight of the body. This could suggest the codes of the lumbar maintain structure, affirm buoyancy, and reveal the codes that truly "hold" us.

Vital organs include the kidneys and the gut.

The gut, known as the "enteric" brain, is a profound hub of emotional and electrical circuitry.

L5
INDEPENDENCE/EXPOSURE

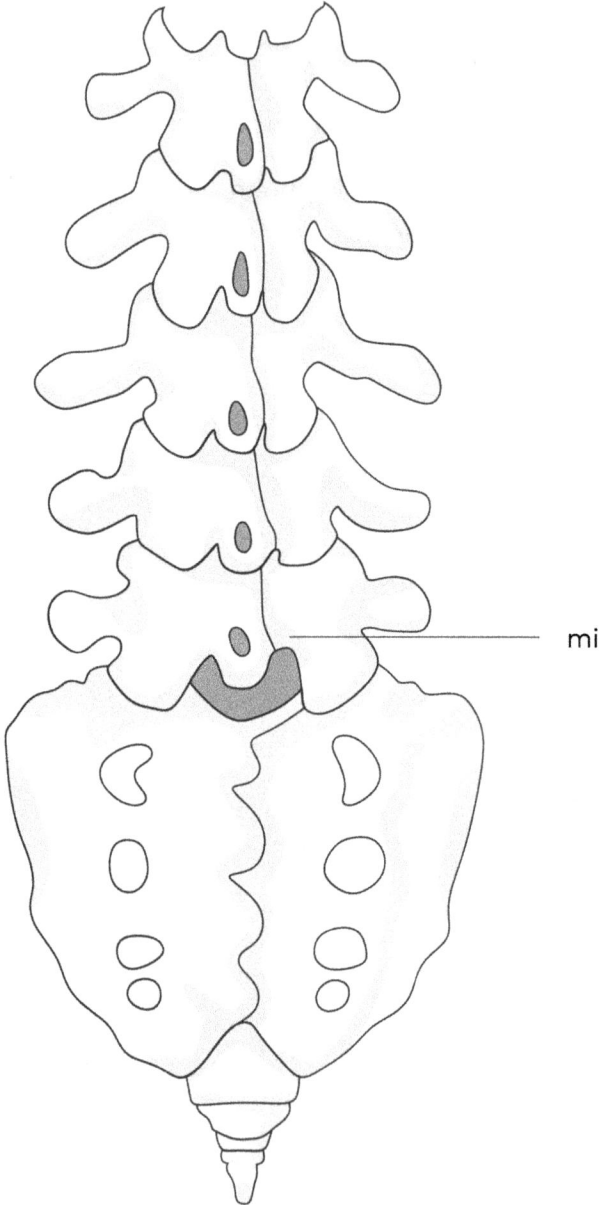

mi

L5 — "MI"

INDEPENDENCE/EXPOSURE

The code of independence involves the important affirmation of self-reliance and personal autonomy. From the diplomacy of S1, there is a significant cessation of the fascination with constant comparison to others. This relentless comparison is what ultimately leads to a cycle of non-essential competition among individuals. When you are freed from the burdensome weight of pathological comparison, you are empowered to resource the inherent tools and strengths that you possess, with true authority. This transformation allows you to be recognized and locatable as a truly unique force in your own right.

Clog: Excessive comparisons

Notes:

L4
INTUITION/INSTINCT

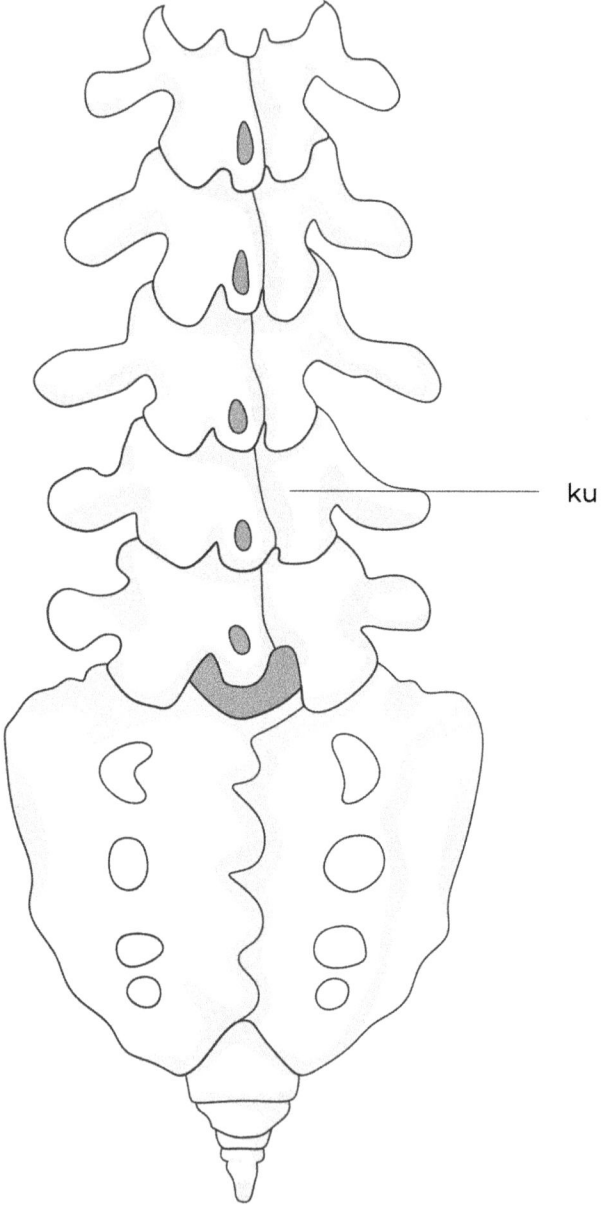

ku

L4 — "KU"

INTUITION/INSTINCT

Intuition and instinct are profound consequences of finding the self just as interesting and compelling as anything that exists in the exterior world. One's sovereign independence and personal agency are not overpowered but rather remain intricately neural in power, enabling a balance with all co-existing forces. All of these co-existing forces are informed by the very same piko, or nucleus, yet exhibit unique and diverse ways in which we translate and interpret the same fundamental essence. Access to this informant, the piko, while maintaining a sense of clarity and not being overpowered by the multitude of translations, represents the true essence of intuition and instinct.

Clog: Distractions

Notes:

L3
INQUIRY

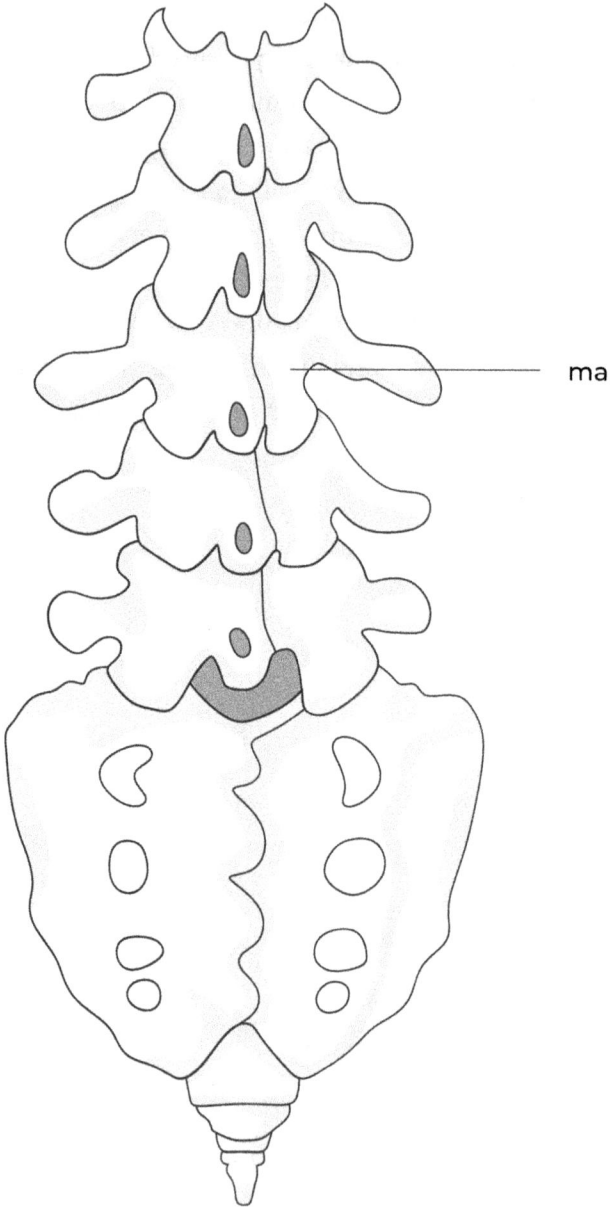

ma

L3 — "MA"

INQUIRY

From the deep authority of intuition, we begin to ask thought-provoking questions. Initially, we pose these insightful questions unto ourselves so that we may effectively refine our answers and understanding. Then, we take this thoughtful design and apply it in an external manner, as we are not attempting to challenge or ridicule others, but rather to support everyone in a collective refinement of our shared answers. This collaborative code is all about the ongoing process of refinement and improvement.

Clog: Self-centeredness

Notes:

L2
EMOTIONAL INTEGRATION

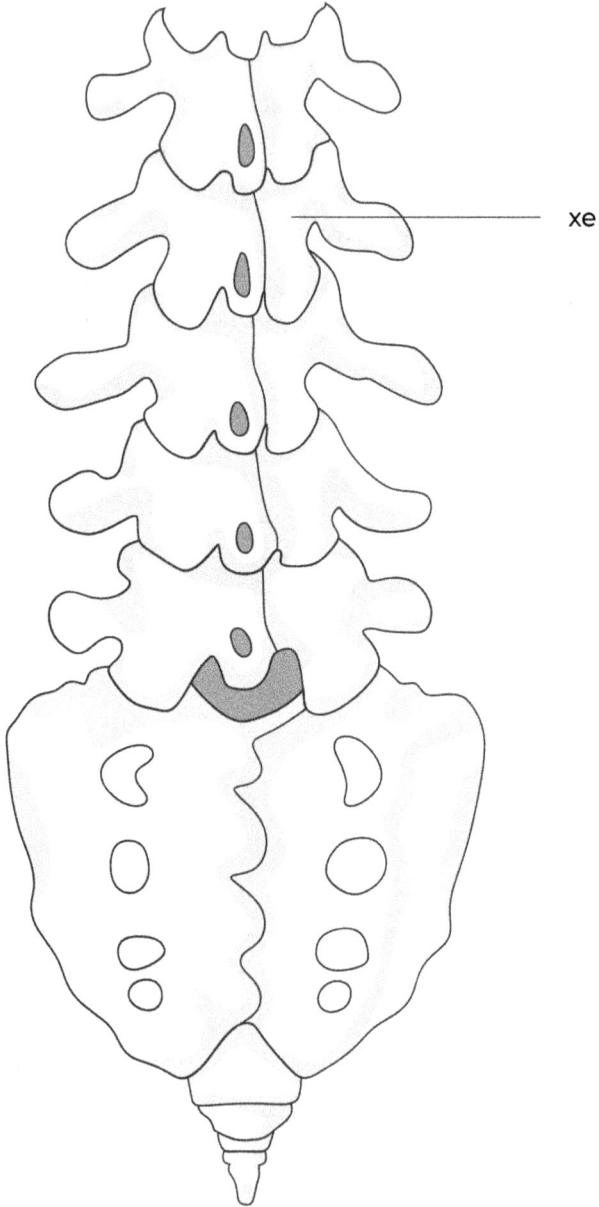

xe

L2 — "XE"

EMOTIONAL INTEGRATION

From refinement of answers, internally and externally, we invite ourselves to feel the voltage of our answers, which also correlates to feeling our decisions in life. This code, L2, invites the play of embodiment so that we can not just feel our answers, but begin to experience how our answers function. This is significant in that L2 is at the precipice of moving into the Thoracic vertebrae, the masculine, who loves the process of functionality.

Clog: Dismissiveness

Notes:

L1
CONFIDENCE/CONVICTION

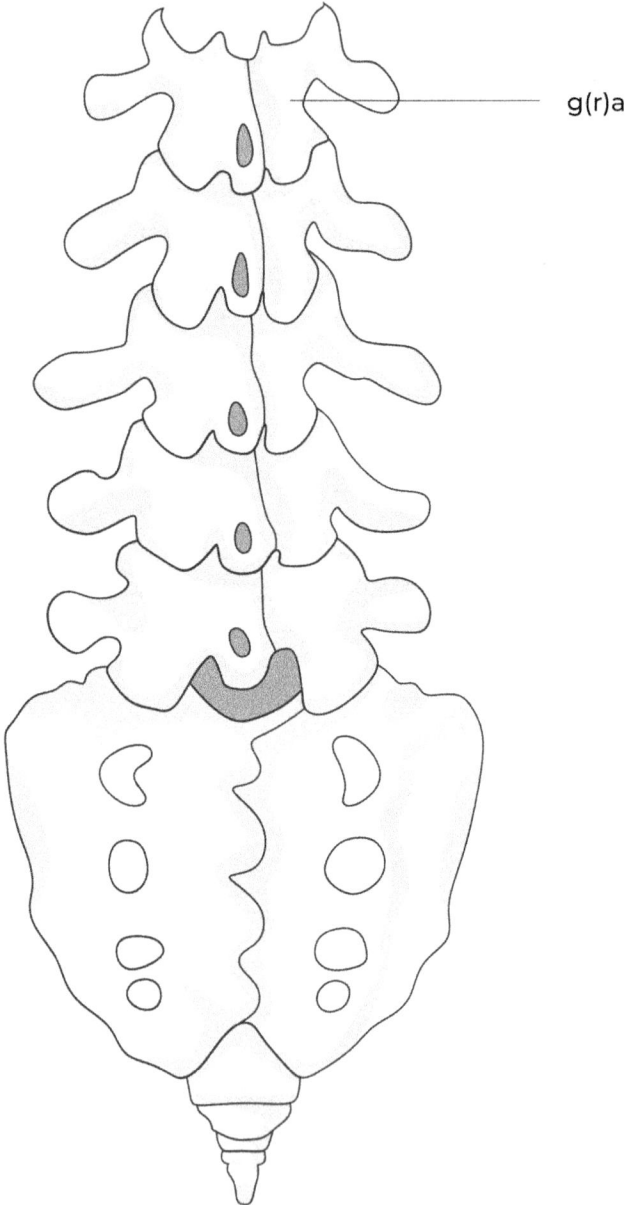

g(r)a

L1 — "G(R)A"

CONFIDENCE/CONVICTION

At the bridge to the thoracic, masculine, we bear the gift of confidence. We know this to be the great dowry the feminine offers her masculine. The 13 codes that bring us to L1, in conjunction with Confidence, becoming 14, is the certainty of one's belonging, and now, we can fully immerse as material. From the safety of inherent belonging, we become artists who play and rejoice in a world of form.

Clog: Insecurity, doubt

Notes:

CHAPTER 4

THORACIC

The 12 vertebrae of the thoracic, also known as the 12 Actions, comprised the internal masculine energetics, the 'Uhane.

Vital organs, such as the lungs, liver, and heart, are associated with the thoracic.

The 12 codes of thoracic comprise the performative, active, and architectural aspects of one's personal capacity. The Thoracic is truly the verb of the self.

The ribcage is unique and specific to the thoracic. The ribcage is symbolic of the actual infrastructure to which the internal masculine, and its 12 actions, produce.

T12
HUMILITY

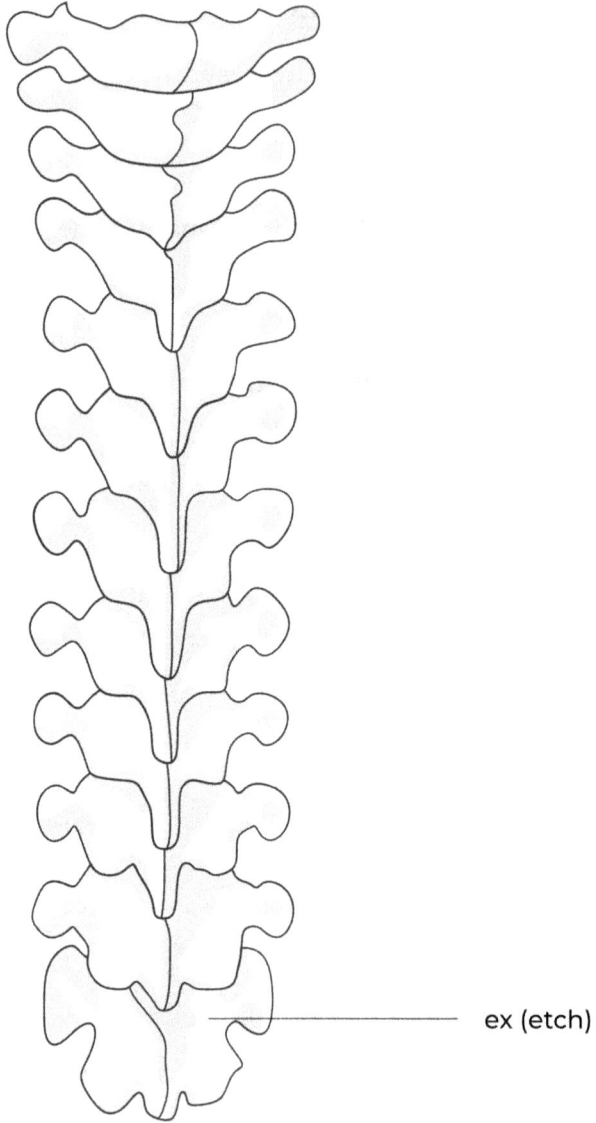

ex (etch)

T12 — "EX" (ETCH)

HUMILITY

The masculine codes open with humility. Humility has histori-cally been translated as being self-aware, receptive, and open to the continuous process of learning. The total of the previous 14 vertebrae, representing the 'Unihipili feminine, is entirely received by the masculine at the critical juncture of T12, which embodies Humility. This essential understanding offers the foundational tools that the masculine will begin to construct, develop, and engineer various forms of infrastructure. In the absence of T12, Humility, the 12 actions of the thoracic region will inevitably need to seek guidance and instructions from external conditions, which may lead to inconsistency.

Clog: Arrogance

Notes:

T11
OBJECTIVES

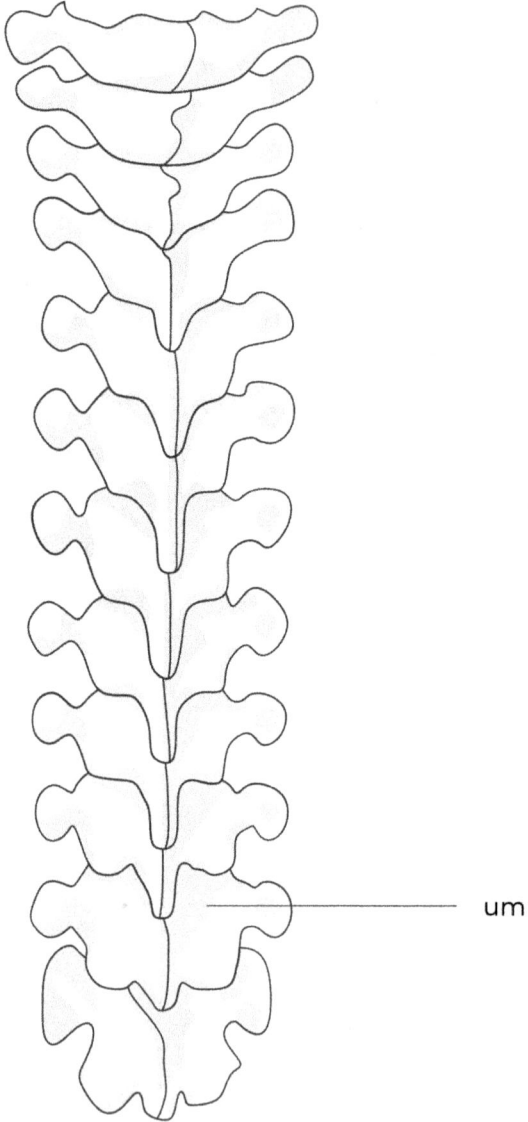

um

T11 — "UM"

OBJECTIVES

The code of Objectives is most simply translated as the question of *what's the plan?* From the very moment of receiving T12, we begin to actively craft, carefully curate, and thoughtfully imagine an actual, comprehensive plan. If the totality of the 'Unihipili complex has been fully and coherently received, then the plan will naturally and effortlessly reveal itself, and T11 is where that begins to take shape.

Clog: Disorganization, incoherence

Notes:

T10
CURIOSITY/INQUIRY

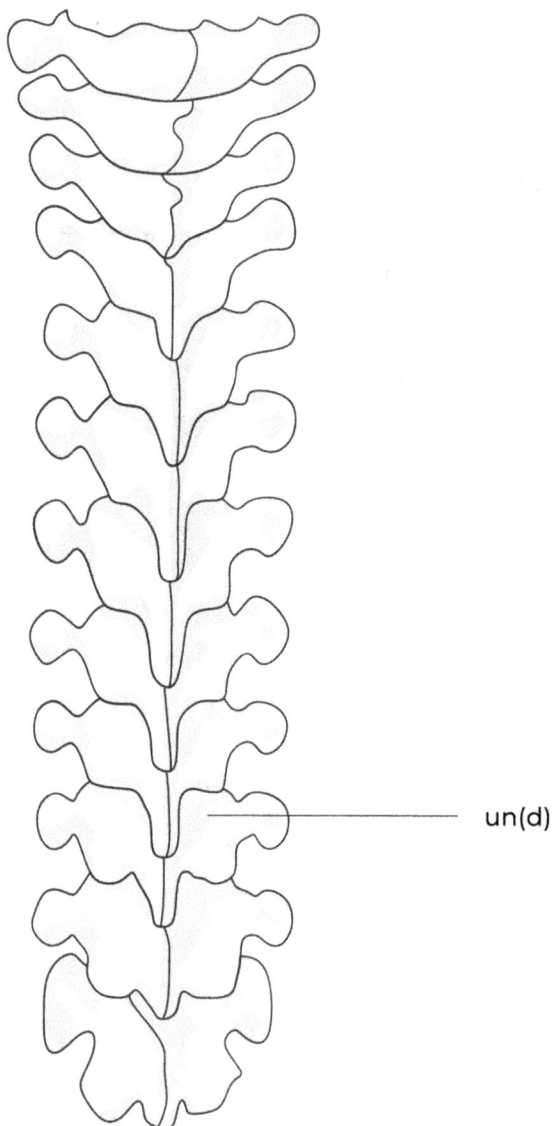

un(d)

T10 — "UN(D)"

CURIOSITY/INQUIRY

Genuine curiosity must be supported by a deep sense of genuine humility, allowing us to be truly receptive to the many variations and contrasting data we encounter. From this foundation of curiosity, we can progress into a thorough and proper assessment, negotiating through all possible avenues to arrive at a well-informed decision. For this reason, T10 initiates our essential skill of negotiation. Mature curiosity plays a vital role in maintaining the necessary flexibility within a negotiation, which in turn ensures that we practice proper diplomacy. This approach effectively prevents the potential rigidity often associated with a suspicious, defensive, and reactive masculine mindset.

Clog: Isolation, intolerant

Notes:

T9
INGENUITY

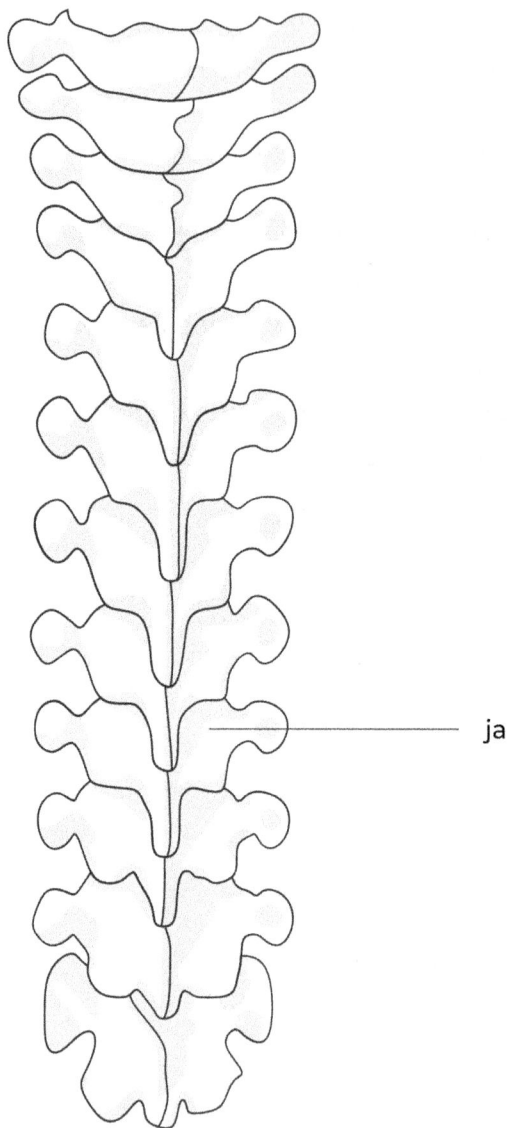

ja

T9 — "JA"

INGENUITY

Genuineness truly lends itself to ingenious potential. Mimicry is, perhaps, one of the most humiliating experiences that can occur within an internal masculine framework. With the valuable support of T9, we are able to remember and rediscover our inherent skills and potential, which are unique to the complex architecture of oneself. This self-awareness fosters a sense of freedom, enabling us to rise above the imposition of external influences that often seek to shape our identity. The authority of one's own principles is firmly affirmed in this space at T9. From this sense of authority, we genuinely begin to experiment with and express our deeply rooted principles.

Clog: Plagiarism, mimicry, fraud

Notes:

T8
ADRENALINE/RHYTHM

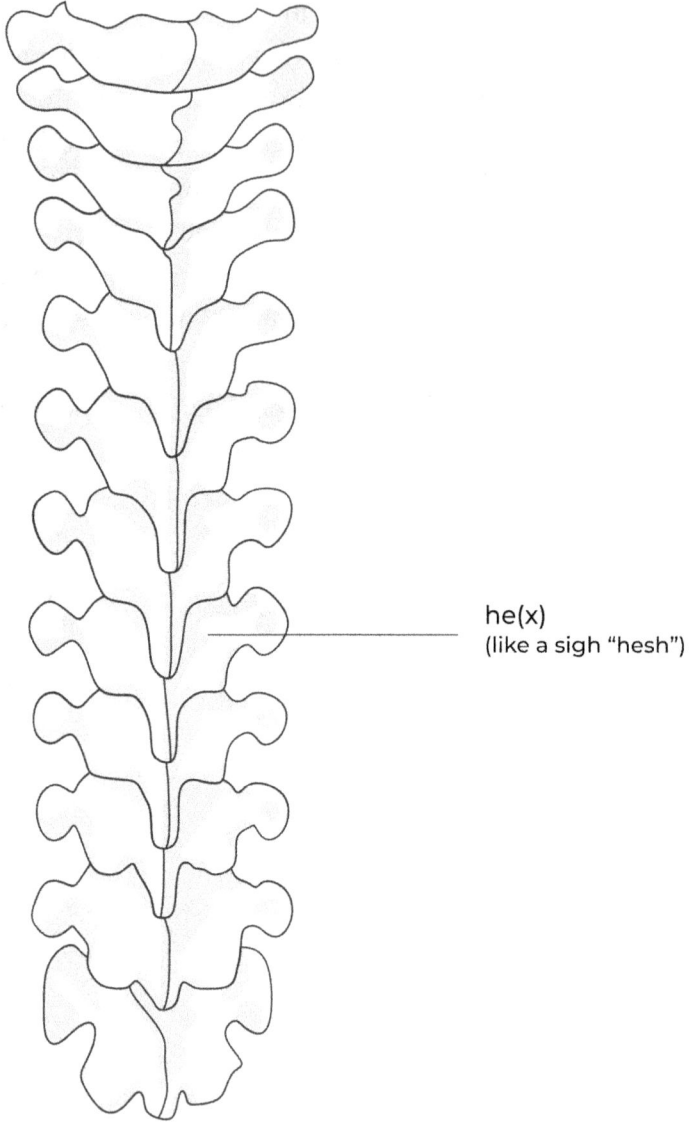

he(x)
(like a sigh "hesh")

T8 — "HE(X)"

ADRENALINE/RHYTHM

The code of T8 brings us into an accelerated state of being, inviting us to explore new dimensions of our existence. This is where the intricate infrastructure of our definition of belonging truly begins to take form and fashion in visible ways. It is the repetition of frequency that creates both the form and structure, while rhythm begins to produce the actual forms that represent the precise frequency at which we are currently functioning, revealing the architecture of our spirit and its relation to the world around us.

Clog: Overwhelm, overstimulation, and/or complacency

Notes:

T7
MIRTH

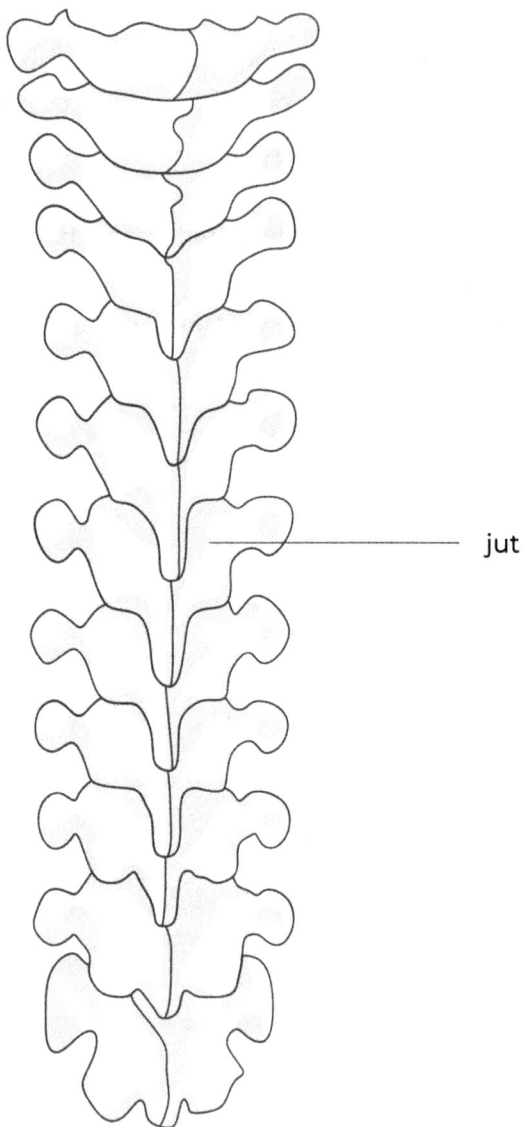

jut

T7 — "JUT"

MIRTH

Mirth. The enjoyment of the condition and activity of one's life. It is at T7, the code of MIRTH, do we truly transition from engineer into artist. The artist finds inspiration in the works. The artist is sensitive and sensual, in relationship with the artifact to which they design. From the code of T8, rhythm, we feel the momentum of productivity as enjoyable and satisfying. That to which we express is adequate, interesting, and exquisite.

Clog: Looking for problems that don't exist.

Notes:

T6
SENSUALITY

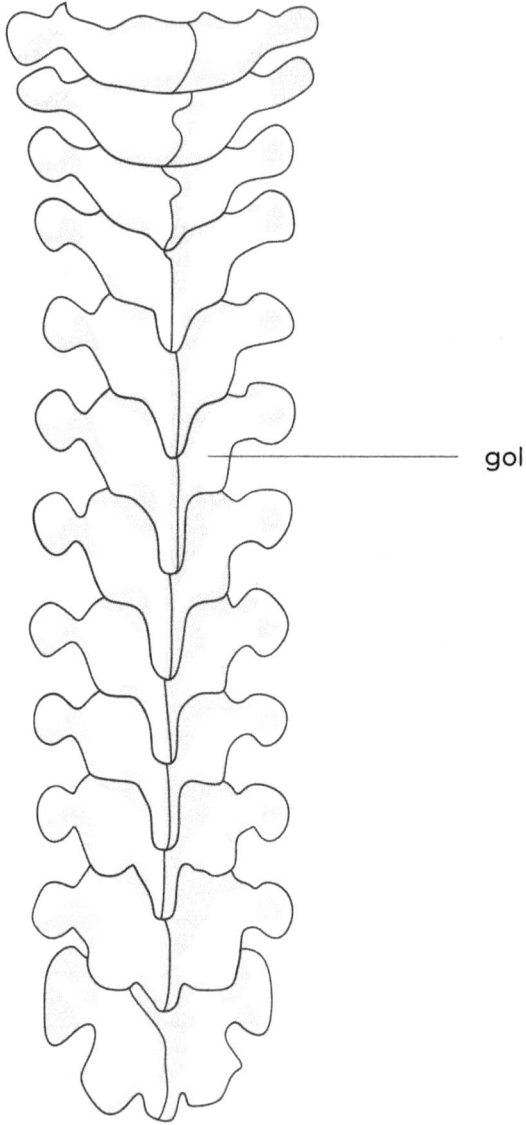

gol

T6 — "GOL"

SENSUALITY

From Mirth, we find a moment to relax and unwind our bodies and minds. In this state of relaxation, we become limber and flexible, allowing for greater tolerance and openness—essential conditions that cultivate sensuality. The code of Sensuality reinstates the permeability we affirm in the 'Unihipili (S3), creating a deeper connection to our inner selves. In the thoracic region, however, the permeability of sensuality is intricately connected to the actual activities we engage in and the design of those experiences. T6 serves as the vital junction through which the inner masculine learns how to gracefully dance through life. From this sensual dance, the masculine energy can be fairly distributed, ensuring that no one part of our being is left under isolating pressure or strain.

Clog: Rigidity, shutting down

Notes:

T5
DEVOTION

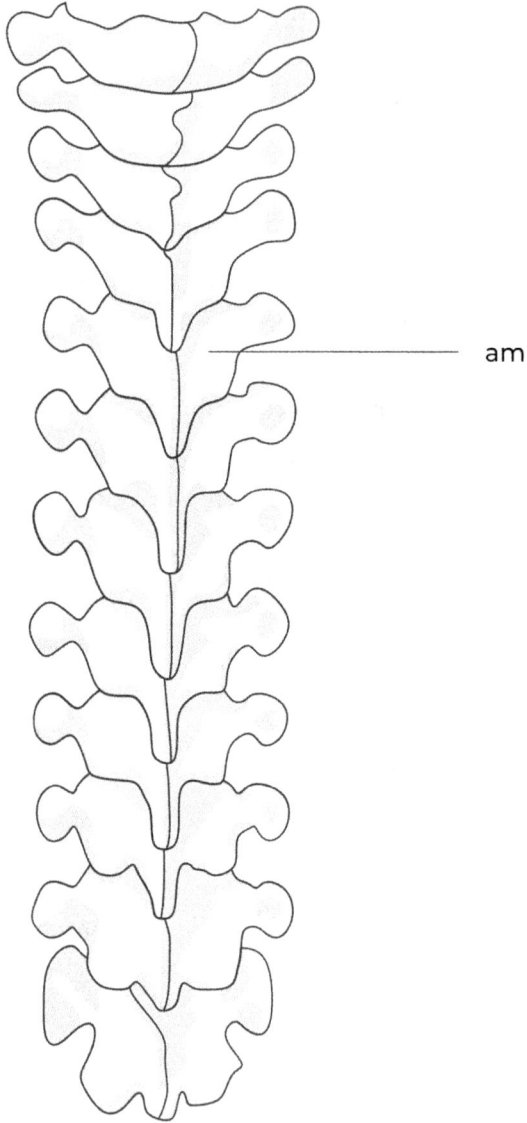

am

T5 — "AM"

DEVOTION

True commitment is the essential code of DEVOTION. The inner masculine, found at T5, is so deeply in love with its engagement in this world that it wholeheartedly selects its position in the ongoing maintenance and enduring support of everything that it is capable of providing. Drawing from the cues of its predecessors, T12-T6, the code of Devotion fully consents to its vital position, embracing the solemn oath to proceed with great joy and unwavering determination.

Clog: Inconsistency, unreliability

Notes:

T4
REPLICATION

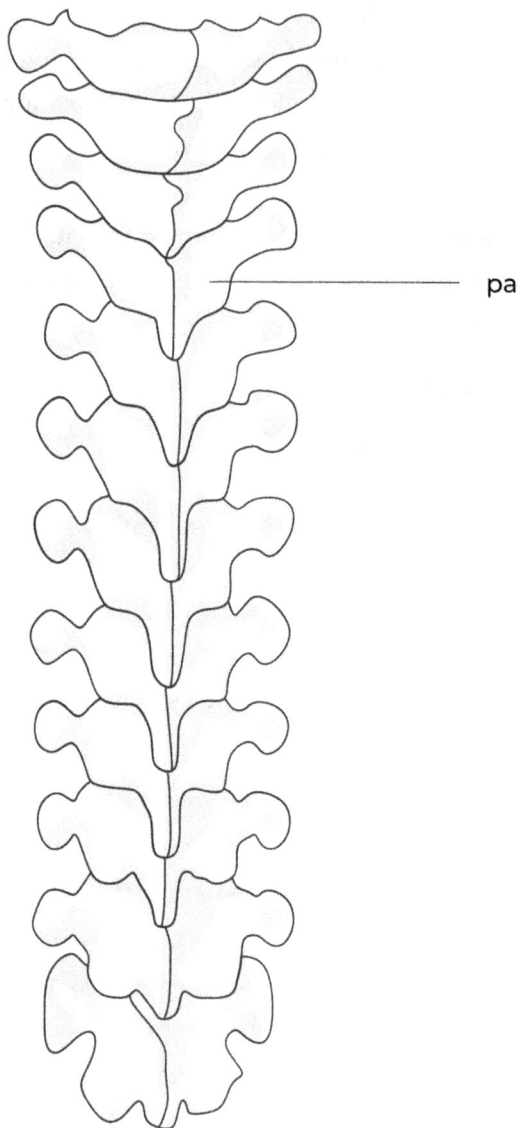

pa

T4 — "PA"

REPLICATION

T4 serves as a reaffirmation of C1, as both concepts inherently share the foundational code of Replication. In the context of T4, we encounter the masculine translation of this notion. In C1, Replication is closely correlated to the basic awareness of sentience and explores how that awareness can manifest itself as a distinct design. In the masculine interpretation of T4, replication signifies the tangible productivity of self-sentience, emphasizing the importance of this productivity as a meaningful contribution. This contribution extends not only to the self but also encompasses the broader external conditions that exist around us. It is at this critical juncture that the individual begins to offer their unique gifts, making them accessible and resourceful for external circumstances. The masculine archetype understands how to share its essence without the fear of depletion; it adeptly replicates itself and its gifts, ensuring these offerings are well-distributed and available to others.

Clog: Hoarding, selfishness

Notes:

T3
PERMEABILITY

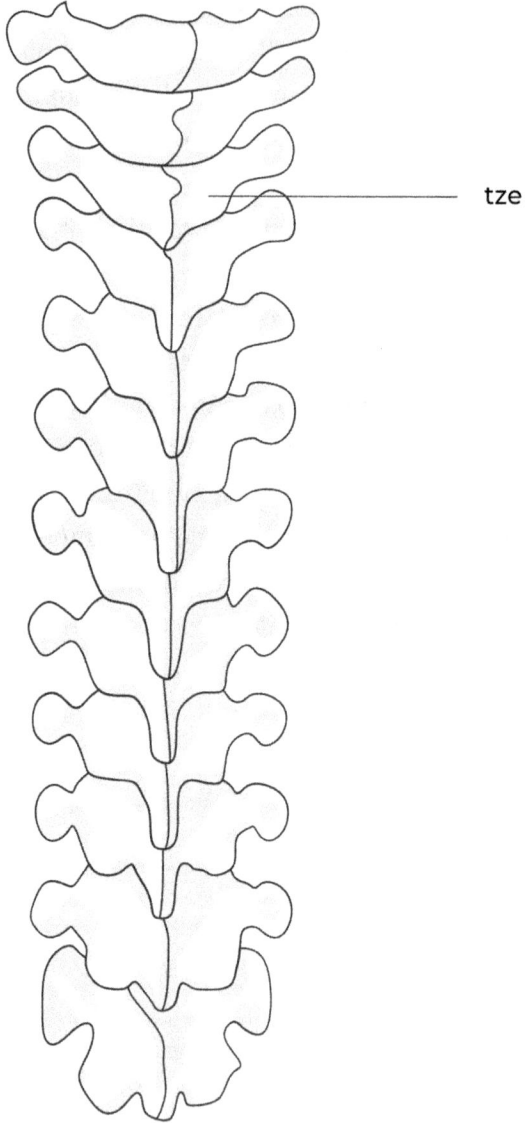

tze

T3 — "TZE"

PERMEABILITY

Like its predecessor, T4, T3 is unified with the previous code of the 'Unihipili complex, S3. In this context, we encounter the distinctive masculine quality of permeability, which plays a crucial role in defining the actual engagement and interaction of contrast and variation with the ever-changing exterior conditions. As a permeable entity, the inner masculine is neither overwhelmed nor overpowered by the presentation of the world surrounding it; instead, it actively collaborates with and thoughtfully contributes to the landscape of experiences it faces.

Clog: Inadequacy caused by comparisons

Notes:

T2
CELEBRATION

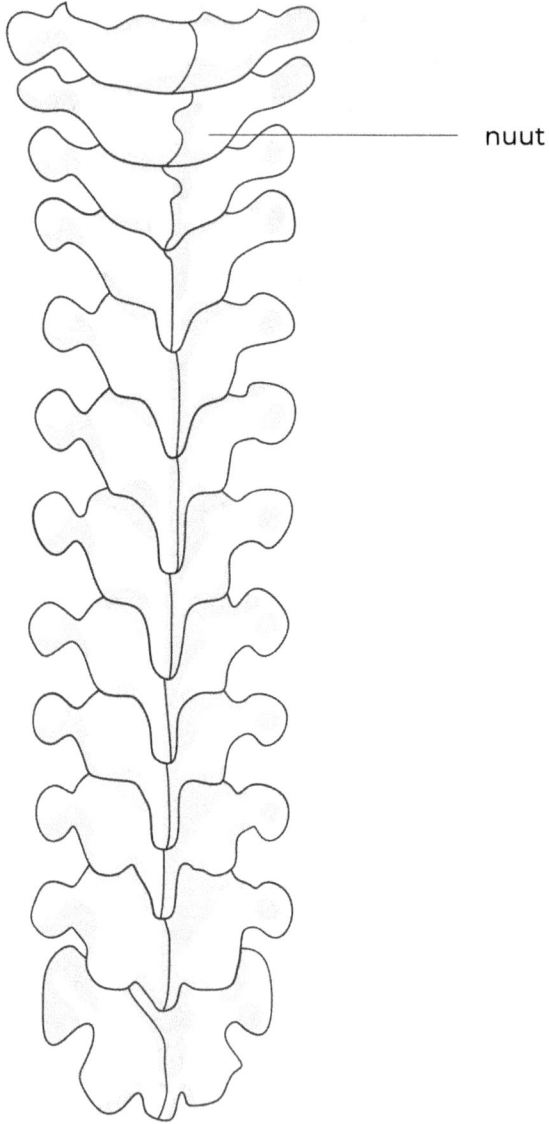

nuut

T2 — "NUUT"

CELEBRATION

Celebratory is the artist who possesses the keen ability to recognize when their work of art is truly complete and accomplished. The second tier can be felt as a profound sense of satisfaction, which deepens the masculine essence into a serene state of relaxation. At this stage, there is no further editing to be made — the artifact is exquisite and stands as a legitimate contribution to the world. From this place of relaxation, the inner masculine experiences a cessation of the relentless intensity of activity, allowing it to simply bear witness to how its meaningful contribution impacts and is received by the world it co-exists within.

Clog: Excess, inability to complete

Notes:

T1
FMOTIONAL RELEASE

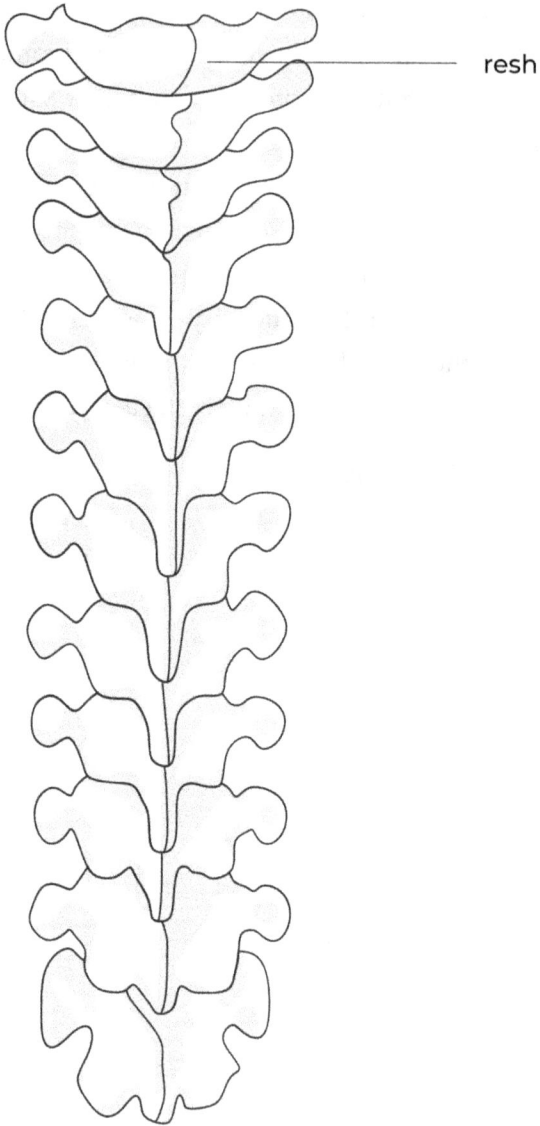

resh

T1 — "RESH"

EMOTIONAL RELEASE

The apex of the masculine experience is the profound notion of Emotional Release. The masculine must release the artistry and the artifact. This journey embraces a sense of non-possession, where true fulfillment lies not in holding tightly to creations but in appreciating their transient beauty. From the code of Celebration, we collectively revel in the positive effects that arise from our creative contributions, while also understanding the importance of simultaneously releasing them back into the universe. For an energy that possesses the potential of becoming heavy and pressurized, the masculine must find joy and delight in the art of emptiness. The expansive pantheon of emotions is both compelling and deeply stimulating. The totality of this sensational exhilaration is offered up and laid upon the altar of human consciousness, serving as a cherished offering to our shared experience. Can the inner masculine truly remember and understand that nothing, and no one, is destined to be a possession?

Clog: Possessiveness, censorship

Notes:

CHAPTER 4

CERVICAL

The sacred 7 vertebrae that comprise the holistic self is the Cervical complex, 'Aumākua.

Seven stages of exultation are coded in C-7 to C-1.

The sacred 7 are the sum of the previous 26 vertebrae in both the 'Uhane and 'Unihipili.

The Cervical includes the brain and its glands and masses.

The pinnacle of the cervical is located hovering 3 inches above the top of the head, *"Manawa."*

C7
INVOLUTION

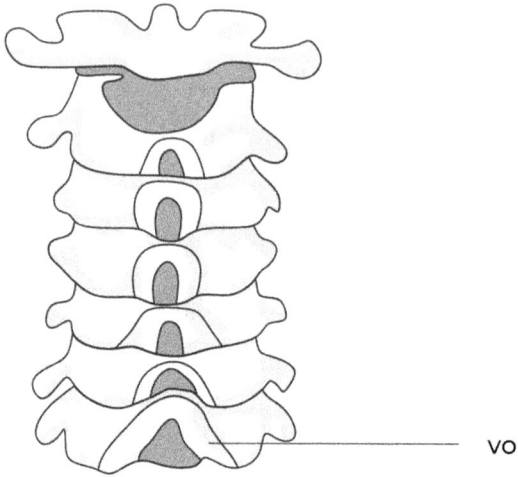

VO

C7 — "VO"

INVOLUTION

The art of Involving is a profound and grand assessment of the total self, encompassing every facet of our being. At C7, we diligently amass all previous codes and begin the comprehensive process of assessment that follows. The key factor in understanding the code of VO is to truly recognize and accept that there is **no further growth to be made**. The intricate process of materialization is complete, and the assembly of the self is finally achieved. As we open up to the Holistic self, Involution celebrates and honors the very definition of holistic: no one individual part can be fully explicable without referencing the whole. Involution represents this whole, and from this profound wholeness, we begin to recognize, appreciate, and marvel at the intricacies of the totally assembled self.

Clog: Fragmentation, dissociation

Notes:

C6
SONG

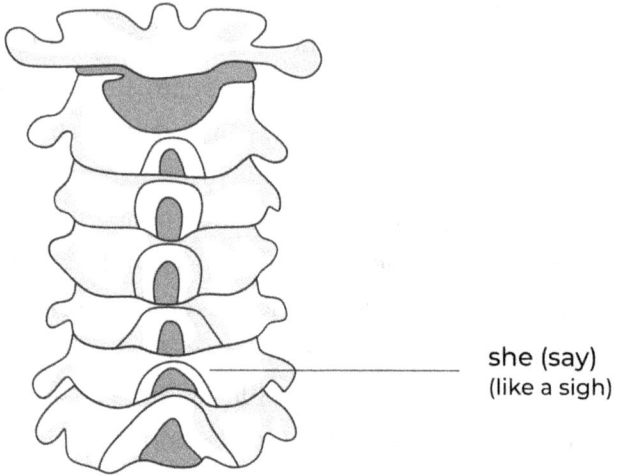

she (say)
(like a sigh)

C6 — "SHE" (SAY)

SONG

The expression of the wholeness of the self, derived from the profound code of involution (C7), is best understood as the SONG itself. Independent of the varying influence, or perhaps even the insistence, of the numerous exterior conditions that may arise, the complete composition, representing the total materialized self, can now fully express, translate, and transfer itself in a meaningful way. This is the essential code in which the sovereign being offers a thoughtful assessment to the exterior world around it. Of course, this process requires that the assessment of the self is not only fully accepted but also genuinely believed in by the self before it can confidently release this treatise. This proclamation, as a song of the self, is a confirmation that the materialization is complete, and the process of Spiritualization is now being requested.

Clog: Withholding

Notes:

C5
MIRACLES

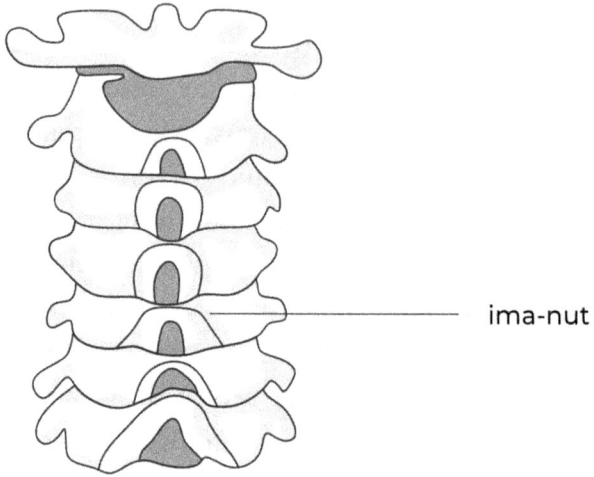

ima-nut

C5 — "IMA-NUT"

MIRACLES

From the genuine expression that occurs during the experience at SONG, a remarkable miracle immediately follows in the form of the *actual reality* that emerges. C5 is the point at which the misguided lens of imitation and mimicry begins to deteriorate, revealing the true reality of one's own perception, which is then fully presented and ultimately recognized. The Actual Reality represents the profound Miracle of C5.

Clog: Mimicry, plagiarism

Notes:

C4
AWE

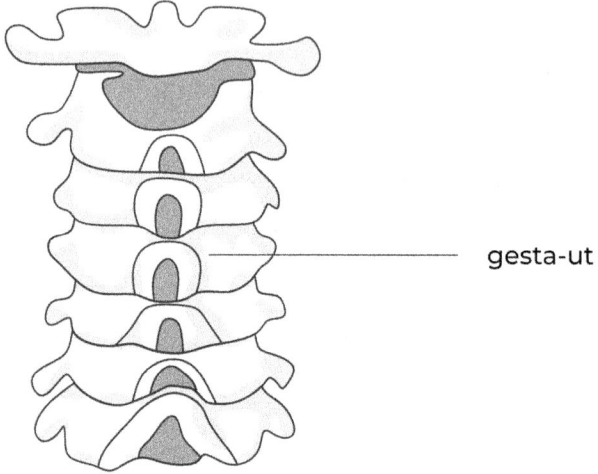

gesta-ut

C4 — "GESTA-UT"

AWE

Blissful is the expansive realm of wonder that is fundamentally achieved in the stage known as C4, Awe. To be truly awestruck by the intricate creation and materialization of the self is not merely a feeling, but rather the energetic and spiritual password that enables the process of Spiritualization to begin. Failing to fulfill a sense of awe regarding the self often indicates that the self is perceived as somehow imperfect, erroneous, or unsatisfied. This perception then informs the process of Materialization, compelling it to either repeat itself or press upon further intricacies of density. Spiritually speaking, this is precisely where the agreement of "reincarnation" is either consented to or declined, marking a significant point in one's spiritual journey.

Clog: Dissatisfaction, scrutiny

Notes:

C3
RELEASE

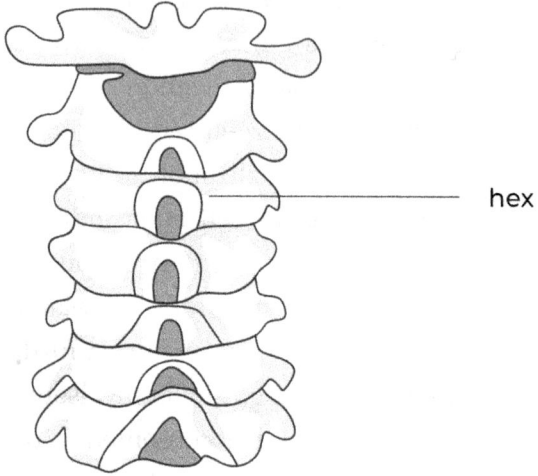

hex

C3 — "HEX"

RELEASE

The realm of the spells, along with the intricate art of spelling, is fully integrated and deeply interconnected. To become truly released from all spells, which includes the powerful spell of Materialization, is a journey that requires engagement and ultimate release. There is no potential, nor any real possibility, of becoming overpowered in this space. The trajectory of one's inherent power is not destined to reach its maximum potential without transfiguration. It is in HEX that we genuinely begin to experience the disintegration of the material form — the gradual scattering of the molecules and cells occurring in a fascinating process of spontaneous evaporation. A spell serves as a directive, and its sole goal is to fulfill its intent. From Awe, the achievement of materialization is wholly affirmed, and the intricate process of material disintegration becomes qualified.

Clog: Obedience

Notes:

C2
TRANSCENDENCE

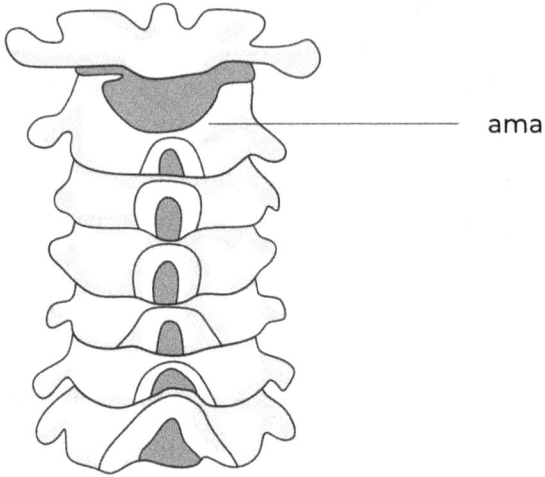

ama

C2 — "AMA"

TRANSCENDENCE

The axis vertebra C2 is considered the code of transcendence. The word axis can beautifully relate to a central point from which various things rotate and align. This spinal code represents the total circumference of the human materialization, encapsulating our physical presence. This essential rotation is what constructs the actual border, or "event horizon," that invites the complete material fullness into the intricate process of spiritualization. From this event horizon, much like the captivating function of a black hole, we begin to feel ourselves dematerialize and transform. A proper "letting go" is now actually occurring, allowing for full recognition of our spiritualization.

Clog: Looking back

Notes:

C1
(THAT WHICH CANNOT BE DESCRIBED)

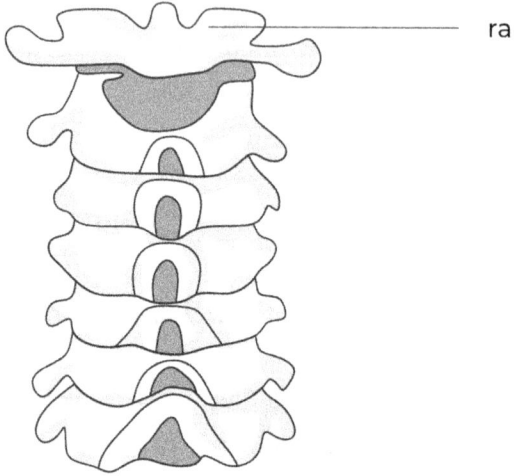

ra

C1 — "RA"

(THAT WHICH CANNOT BE DESCRIBED)

Cervical 1 is widely recognized as the atlas vertebrae. The term "Atlas" has historically been translated to mean a book of maps or charts, symbolizing a vital reference point. We can interpret the code of RA as a representation of the totality, the whole, encapsulated within the concept of Akasha, presented in its complete and intricate composition and compilation. This is the actual metaphorical book that is transformed into the next expression as the material self undergoes a profound spiritualization process. It is important to note that no physical form or material can be directly transferred. Instead, only the compilation and composition of the Akasha that constitutes the essence of the self is transferable. This concept is encapsulated within the code of RA. At the moment we reach C1, all brain glands and masses are fully activated, and the charge, or voltage, present is so immense that it creates a sudden combustion. This combustion, in tandem with the rhythmic cessation of the heart, qualifies the unique wormhole, black hole, or passage through which we transfer, completely and entirely. Essentially, the material consumes itself.

Clog: Identity

Notes:

CHAPTER 5
THE MECHANICS

In 'ULU, active participation and meaningful collaboration with the physical body serve as foundational elements in our practice. Through the art of 'ULU, we fully immerse ourselves in the intricate relationship we have with our physical body; we engage in a process of remembering how to communicate effectively with the body, how to alchemize our experiences, and to rearrange our internal landscapes. It is not completely unrealistic to think that we can edit various components and qualities of our physical structure as a result of our growing fluency in 'ULU. It is important to note that the proficiency of the body does not necessarily imply that one must always be in motion; rather, sometimes, the essence of the relationship is found in the act of deep observing of the body. This is one of the key objectives that ULU strives to accomplish — to offer us a unique lens through which we can see from both the outside in and the inside out. This practice encourages us to notice and inform the patterns within the physical structure as well as the energetic particulars that make up our complex electrical makeup. Movement, then, emerges from a place of careful observation and reflection. In this context, movement becomes secondary to the understanding we gain. The techniques of 'ULU, referred to as "designs," allow us to resource the physical body in order to create distinct patterns that, when applied with consistency, formulate a reliable point of convergence for our energies. For this reason, we can attribute the movement designs of 'ULU — which include various breathing designs — to the creation of momentary portals that magnetize our essence or open up transformative spaces within ourselves. This phenomenon is particularly evident in the opening of the vertebrae of the spinal column, where the codes that become accessible can profoundly inform a true composition of the self in relation to a material world, enriching our overall experience and enjoyment.

In the proper application of 'ULU, we have a series of protocols that ensure compatibility of practice. I will summarize this protocol, step by step, to offer you a glimpse into this exquisite orientation.

1ST PROTOCOL: KŪLIKE

Kūlike is widely regarded as the most archaic expression found within the rich culture of Mū. It involves the intentional placement of the left hand upon the sacral region and the right hand positioned over the heart. Throughout various regions in Polynesia, as well as South America and Africa, we discover ancient relics, preserved in stone, that depict this significant pose. For my lineage, whenever we encounter this specific representation, we instinctively recognize that the relic originates from Mū. The term Kūlike itself translates to stand tall, which intricately refers to maintaining the energetic upright posture with a strong focus on the integrity and erectness of the spinal cord, often likened to an obelisk.

In the practice of Kūlike, our backbone is not only supported but also empowered as we move forward to engage with anything or anyone, including the self. Furthermore, Kūlike holds the esteemed position of being the very first step in a traditional 'ULU practice. When this fundamental step is performed in solitude, the individual is, in essence, greeting themselves in a state of energetic integrity, fostering a deeper connection with their inner self, thus activating the aliveness of the codes of the spinal code.

Instructions:

In the ceremony of *Kūlike*, we:

1. Raise the right hand. This is the recognition of the internal masculine, thoracic vertebrae.
2. Then, we place the right hand over the heart, the pu'uwai.
3. We inhale through the nose and hold.
4. As we hold our breath, we apply the oxygen in the heart-space, we share breath with our internal 'Uhane.
5. We exhale. In the exhalation, the hā, we feel our 'uhane relax. In this relaxation, our masculine is removed of urgency and hostility and restored as the Hero.
6. We offer a mantra of the masculine: *Pā Wale Pu'uwai (open your heart wider)*

Keeping the right hand over the heart, we raise the left hand.

1. In the raising of the left, we are in recognition of the internal feminine, the coccyx, sacral, and lumbar.
2. Then, we place the left hand over the na'au, the sacral.
3. We inhale through the nose and hold.
4. As we hold our breath, we apply the oxygen in the sacral, we share breath with our internal 'Unihipili.
5. We exhale. In the exhalation, the hā, we feel our 'unihipili expand. In this expansion, our feminine is removed from obscurity and neglect and restored to Faith.
6. We offer a mantra of the feminine: *Ua Malu (I am safe)*

With both hands in the proper position known as Kūlike, a moment of pause as to integrate the Right Relation between:

The noun and the verb.

The intention, and the manifestation.

The dream and the action.

Quantum and linear.

The leader, the hero.

Belonging and infrastructure

This coalescing results in the energy of 'Aumākua — the holistic, androgynous, self — and honors the sacred 7 of the cervical vertebrae. Now, the whole self is fully present.

ALOHA MĀ.

2ND PROTOCOL: RECITATION OF THE 33 TONES, 3 TIMES.

The individual will recite the 33 tones three distinct times in a deliberate manner, as this is necessary to effectively strum the spinal cord, thereby preparing for the enlightening 'ULU design.

On the first recitation, we begin our journey at the coccyx, specifically at C4, and carefully tone ourselves upward to reach the axis of Cervical 1. In this initial recitation, the primary intention is to *unlock* all 33 vertebrae along the spinal column. It is quite possible that the individual may remain unconscious of any potential locking or shutting down of specific vertebrae, or even the entire spinal cord as a whole. Beginning with the C4 vertebra, I set my intention and gave my consent to fully unlock the entirety of my spinal cord.

Immediately following this process of unlocking, we gather our focus once again at the coccyx 4, or tailbone, in preparation for the second recitation of the 33 codes.

During the second recitation, we proceed by strumming up from Coccyx 4 to Cervical 1. Here, the primary intention shifts to PLUGGING IN. We work to adapt each singular vertebra to the vast fabric of Akasha, so that it may channel and transfer its unique code without any form of obstruction. It is essential to recognize that the individual may also be unconscious of any potential misfiring that can occur at specific vertebrae or along the entire spinal cord as a unit.

As we transition to the third phase, we must now focus on GROUNDING the experience that we have cultivated. For the third installation, we reverse our approach, starting with our focus at Cervical 1 and then strumming our way down through the entire cord until we reach the coccyx 4 once more. The primary intention during this phase is to GROUND the voltage that has manifested within our activated spinal cord. The art of grounding is fundamental in ensuring that all expressions that emerge from the spinal cord during the 'ULU design process are transferrable, relatable, and made practical in everyday life. If the process of grounding, for anything, is not properly respected and honored, we risk becoming overwhelmed or overpowered by those energies that channel through us.

Coccyx

CO4 "KA" (pronounced *kah*)
CO3 "LU" (pronounced *lou*)
CO2 "KO" (pronounced *koe*)
CO1 "HA" (pronounced *ha*)

Sacrum

S5 "LI" (pronounced *lee*)
S4 "ONE" (pronounced *own*)
S3 "HI" (pronounced *hee*)
S2 "WA" (pronounced *vah*)
S1 "I" (pronounced *e*)

Lumbar

L5 "MI" (pronounced *me*)
L4 "KU" (pronounced *koo*)
L3 "MA" (pronounced *mah*)
L2 "XE" (pronounced *shay*)
L1 "G(r)A" (pronounced *gara*)

Thoracic

T12 "EX" (pronounced *etch*)

T11 "UM" (pronounced *oom*)

T10 "UN(d)" (pronounced *oond*)

T9 "JA" (pronounced *jah*)

T8 "HE(x)" (pronounced *hesh*, uttered as a sigh)

T7 "JUT" (pronounced *jooht*)

T6 "GOL" (pronounced *goal*)

T5 "AM" (pronounced *ahm*)

T4 "PA" (pronounced *pah*)

T3 "TZE" (pronounced *tzh*)

T2 "NUUT" (pronounced *nout*)

T1 "RESH" (pronounced *resh*)

Cervical

C7 "VO" (pronounced *vou*)

C6 "SHE" (pronounced *say*, uttered as a sigh)

C5 "IMA-NUT" (pronounced *e-mah-noot*)

C4 "GESTA-UT" (pronounced *gay-stah-oot*)

C3 "HEX" (pronounced *hex*)

C2 Axis "AMA" (pronounced *ah-mah*)

C1 Atlas "RA" (pronounced *rah*)

3RD PROTOCOL: THE HOE

Modern Hawaiian will translate Hoe as *"to inhale and sigh," "to endure the work."* However, the word Hoe is a very old term that details the breathing and vocal inclusion of 'Ulu.

'Ulu is not just a movement art; it also includes breath and sound.

One part of the activation and stimulation of the spinal cord is the distributing potential of our breath.

The Hoe functions as an *activator*.

Hoe is commonly honored before the actual movement part of 'Ulu as to ensure the entire physical and auric field is present. Hoe also ensures that presence is properly distributed throughout the whole system. Basic breathing techniques achieve this — feel the vocal part as coming into leadership of the process, directing and informing.

There are 3 basic, and fundamental, Hoe correlating to the spinal cord:

1. 'Unihipili (Coccyx, sacral, lumbar)

The breath and sound of "HXE" (pronounced like a cat's hiss).

For this Hoe, as you utter, you will consolidate tension in your sacral and your gut, the enteric brain. You will also feel tension in the sexual organs. This can be likened to the feminine bringing all things into a nucleus, applying pressure, and creating a diamond. In the vocal utterance, you may also experience a complete expulsion of breath, emptying. The way I experience this, personally, is like a cleaning and sweeping of my physical and auric fields.

2. 'Uhane (Thoracic)

The breath and sound of "TAY" (lit. "tay" like a rapid sigh).

For this hoe, the concentration is at the heart space. As you utter Tay, you arch your back, pulling the heart forward. Feel it as though you are resurrecting the beat of a heart. All energetics will converge at the heart, and as you pull your chest forward, we are not only activating the heart, we are also propelling and compelling it.

3. 'Aumākua (Cervical)

The breath and sound of "HA" (lit. "Ha", like a sigh of relief)

For this hoe, the focus is on the third eye and crown. All energetics have converged to this apex where, with the sound of HA, as a signal, your crown opens and all is released. This can be likened to a sensation of becoming unburdened. Upon the utterance, you feel your entire body relax, but remain upright due to the immense energy that is released at the crown, behaving like an invisible string holding you up.

As the third and final protocol preceding a formal 'Ulu design, the HOE meticulously distributes the intricate circuitry of the spinal cord across all parts of the physical body, while simultaneously extending its influence as the auric field. This innovative bio-psychic technology is experienced as the tangible curating of one's personal atmosphere. As the atmosphere becomes fully present, it now holds the physical and holistic body in a harmonious state of buoyancy. As levitation is recognized as a primary code of conduct for achieving homeostasis, the HOE effectively generates the necessary voltage and heightened awareness, allowing the spinal cord to extend itself, energetically, beyond the confines of the actual physical body, manifesting as the expansive auric field that ultimately becomes the very atmosphere of the self.

CHAPTER 6
THE DESIGNS

In this comprehensive guidebook, we will share with you three fundamental ULU designs that form an essential part of our exploration. These specific designs are just a small selection from the vast known total of approximately 12,000 variations. Ōnū is uniquely tailored to the activation and engagement of the 'Unihipili complex, highlighting its significance. Laulā is particularly specific for the 'Uhane, emphasizing its distinct attributes. Lastly, Hū serves as a powerful design that relates to the cervical 'Aumākua, connecting various dimensions of practice. When proficiency is achieved in all three designs, they collectively transform into a unified 'Ulu design in its own right. The oscillation created through honoring this unification emerges as a remarkably effective method of attaining a holistic and cohesive 'Ulu practice.

ŌNŪ, "TO MAXIMIZE"

In *Ōnū*, our inherent feminine, 'Unihipili, remembers how to uncoil and sprawl her wings. This is a radical call to become removed from confinement and obscurity. Ōnū is the liberation of the autonomy and belonging of the inherent feminine.

Focus is uniquely centered with the hands at the tailbone area, front and back of the body, as we unlock, and then fling with the arms, drawing open the expansiveness of the wing span. We are consenting the feminine to uncoil its wings and soar once again. This simple 'Ulu design has three essential steps. We recommend sitting cross-legged, or on your knees, ensure your immediate environment affords you lots of space to move freely.

Instructions:

1. Place your left hand on your tailbone, palm facing away from the body.

2. Keeping your left hand where it is, bring your right hand to the front of your belly, palm facing in toward the body.

3. Fling both hands outward in opposite directions, using the full force of your arms.

Reverse:

1. Place your right hand on your tailbone, palm facing away from the body.

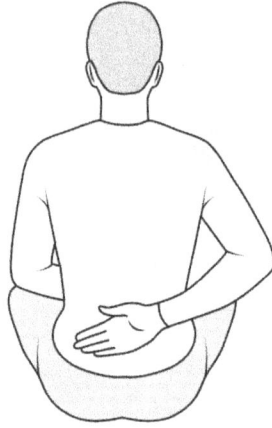

2. Keeping your right hand where it is, bring your left hand to the front of your belly, palm facing in toward the body.

3. Fling both hands outward in opposite directions, using the full force of your arms.

Keep reversing in succession, creating a continuous oscillation.

The key is to always begin with your left hand. If you choose to place your left hand at the front instead, just be sure your right hand moves to the back — the hands must always mirror each other.

You may also notice that the speed of this process naturally encourages you to fuse steps 1 and 2 into one fluid motion — as if you're scraping the front and back of your body just before flinging your arms outward in step 3. This integration is both expected and appropriate within the rhythm of Ōnū.

With each distinct step, feel free to enhance your movements with a vocal expression — such as Hoe, the third protocol introduced in Chapter 4. While performing Ōnū, you can honor the sound *"hxe"* in step 1, *"tay"* in step 2, and *"ha"* in step 3. Play with this dynamic. Let your body and voice move together. Most importantly, trust what resonates deeply within you as you honor the established protocol of three.

Upon completing your unique design, with eyes gently closed (or with your eye covering still in place), it is recommended to place your left hand over your sacral region and your right hand over your heart. This supports the integration of your experience in alignment with Kūlike, the first protocol introduced in Chapter 4.

Inwardly gaze towards the drip of your spinal fluids, or you may become increasingly aware of the oscillation of the Wat-eht. Only open your eyes, or remove your eye covering, once you have completed and honored your integration.

This particular design, although it may appear simple at first glance, is considered to be of intermediate difficulty due to the degree of challenge it may present. Sustaining the flinging motion of the arms for extended durations can prove to be quite challenging and may require significant effort.

Therefore, if you find that you must take a moment to rest your arms, it is helpful to maintain the rhythm of the design by softly uttering the syllables of the Hoe — "hxe," "tay," and "ha." With each utterance, direct your inward gaze and visualize the actual fluid movements as they flow. For instance, at the sound of "ha," take a moment to visualize the flinging motion of step 3, and immerse yourself in the sensation of your wings uncoiling and extending freely. Additionally, you may want to create your own modification for these intermittent rest periods to better suit your comfort. The invitation is to dedicate to a design that lasts at least 30 minutes, non-stop. You can begin by experimenting with 15 minutes and gradually build toward 30 minutes.

Ultimately, it can be quite fun to honor a proper 'Ulu design of 60 minutes, uninterrupted.

LAULĀ, "THE WIDTH OF LIBERATION"

As the width of liberation, the design of *Laulā* is intentionally crafted to honor the intricate geometry of the inherent masculine, located in the 'Uhane thoracic vertebrae. Through continued exploration and understanding, we have come to recognize the thoracic 'Uhane as the essential aspect of our being responsible for building, designing, and maintaining the infrastructures of life. This is intriguingly and evidently expressed through what we refer to as *The 12 Actions*.

The design of Laulā exquisitely highlights the masculine's deep love and appreciation for the principles of geometry. The hands and arms, in their methodical and deliberate movements, gracefully trace the symbol of the cross at the midline of the body. This potent cross, which predates Christianity, is uniquely attributed to the expression of masculine energy and invites a deeper understanding of its significance.

Instructions:

1. Bring your left hand to your heart space, palm facing right, resting along the centerline of the body.

2. Bring your right hand to meet it, palm facing left, so that both hands come together in a prayer position at the heart.

3. In simultaneous motion, fling both hands upward, reaching as far as the arms can extend above the head.

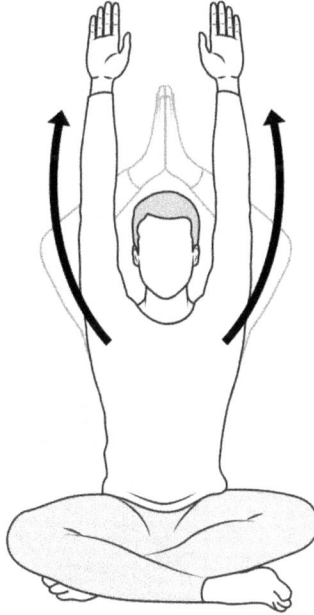

4. Return the left hand to the heart space, palm facing right, while keeping the right hand lifted.

4. Bring the right hand back to the heart space, palm facing left, returning to the prayer position.

4. In simultaneous motion, push the hands in opposite directions, turning the palms to face outward, and extend the arms fully until they reach their maximum width.

You are encouraged to utter the Hoe at each interval.

At Step 1, when the left hand shifts to the heart, honor the sound *"hxe."*

At Step 2, when the right hand shifts to the heart, honor the sound *"tay."*

At Step 3, when the arms fling up, honor the sound *"ha."*

At Step 4, when the left hand returns to the heart, honor the sound *"hxe."*

At Step 5, when the right hand follows, honor the sound *"tay."*

At Step 6, when the arms press outward to full width, complete the cycle with the sound *"ha."*

Begin with a full oscillation for 5 minutes. Then pause. Integrate. Once your body adjusts, challenge yourself to extend to 10 minutes. Pause again. Integrate. In time, allow yourself to flow uninterrupted for 30 to 60 minutes, non-stop.

When you complete your design, be sure to bring your hands into Kūlike for proper integration. If you choose to lie down, you may still place your hands in Kūlike to complete the sequence.

As with any other 'Ulu design, if your arms need rest, simply maintain the Hoe to keep the oscillation moving along the spinal cord. And if you must pause the Hoe, for example if your throat becomes dry, continue the movement. Sometimes it's helpful to volley between sound and motion, which can promote much longer durations of Laulā.

Remember: We are creating the symbol of The Cross. This is symbolic of retrieving the unseen information and transferring it into the infrastructure. This is truly what the cross represents: the merging of the seen and the unseen.

As you engage in this intricate design process, be ma'a (aware) of both the subtle and larger dynamics that are occurring, as well as what you are consciously consenting to throughout this journey. Your fluency with the 33 codes invites a deeper understanding of how to manifest proper form and infrastructure, as determined by the unique actions you choose to take.

When the arms pull apart in step 6, we are effectively widening the capacity to bring this essential information into tangible form. Conversely, when we lift the arms upwards, we are actively cracking open that precious access to exultation and joy. The masculine energy serves as the vital bridge that connects the 'Unihipili (alpha) with the 'Aumākua (omega), establishing a profound link between these two realms.

HŪ, "TO OVERFLOW"

Erupting vigorously from the crown, the *"manawa,"* representing the pure energy of our holistic self at its ultimate overflow, pours unto itself and extends generously as a meaningful contribution to all beings around us.

The extraordinary power of the ʻAumākua, the cervical vertebrae comprising the exalted seven, embodies the profound essence of Spiritualization.

As the hands gently touch the top of the head, they invite and consent to the voltage of the holistic energy to erupt.

As the open palms gradually descend along the measure of the body, at both ends, we find ourselves basking in our own glory.

In this moment, the medicine of the self is fully actualized, allowing the transformative process of Spiritualization to commence in a harmonious way.

Hū is a very simple design.

In tandem with the HOE...

Instructions:

1. Begin seated, with both hands resting on your legs, palms facing up.

2. Place your left hand over the crown of your head, palm facing down, cupped. You may choose to let the hand hover about three inches above the head, or gently rest it directly on the crown. Utter *"hxe"*.

3. Place your right hand, over the crown of your head, palm facing down, cupped, and lay it on top of the left hand. Utter *"tay"*.

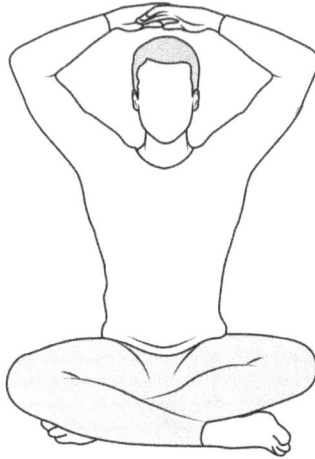

4. Extend, open, and drop both arms down in simultaneous motion, like a fountain. As you swing your arms down, you'll notice the downward-facing palms naturally rotate upward, forming the shape of a cup. Let the hands swing all the way down to your hips. Utter "hā".

Repeat, repeat, repeat.

Like all other 'Ulu designs, it is important to titrate yourself so that you are effectively committed to the Hū process for a period of up to 30 to 60 minutes, without any interruptions or breaks.

Similar to other designs, if you feel that your arms are in need of rest, make sure that you are still uttering the Hoe mantra while concentrating on each breath in conjunction with the appropriate step.

At Step 2, when uttering "hxe", channel your inward focus toward the intentional cupping of your hand over the top of your head.

At Step 3, when uttering "tay", maintain a committed focus on your right hand as it shields the left hand, ensuring a strong sense of balanced protection.

Lastly, during Step 4, when uttering "hā", direct focused attention toward the imagery of a fountain that erupts energetically from the crown of your head.

ŌNU, LAULĀ, HŪ: IN COMBINATION

From the proper fluency and proficiency of all three intricate designs, seamlessly merge them into one cohesive, holistic design.

Start with the uncoiling and flinging of the wings at Ōnū, which transitions gracefully into the geometry of Laulā. From the extended arms at the end of Laulā, flow directly into Hū.

Beginning with Ōnū, place your left hand on the tailbone, palm facing outward, and your right hand on the belly/sacral area. Fling both hands outward in opposite directions, using the full force of your arms.

Entering into Laulā, bring the left hand to the front of the heart, along the centerline of the body, while the right hand meets it in a prayerful gesture. Fling both hands upward in unison before returning them to prayer position at the heart.

Then, simultaneously open your arms wide to flow into Hū, shifting the left hand to the top of the head to create a gentle cup, followed closely by the right hand covering the left — simulating an opening that creates the overflow of a fountain.

As both hands gracefully cascade down toward the ground and come to rest by the sides of the body, marking the completion of Hū, smoothly transition back into Ōnū by placing the left hand on the tailbone and the right hand on the belly/sacral area.

Continue to repeat this sequence.

Through the precision of this combined trinity design, you may begin to feel the true essence of the Wat-Eht start to invigorate you. The subtle drip of brain fluids may become apparent as you sense their journey up and down the spinal cord.

Enjoy the experience!

CHAPTER 7
THE SPIRITUALIZATION AND ALOHA MĀ

Spiritualization emerges as a profound consequence of materialization. The most obvious and readily apparent aspect of the human experience is undeniably our physical body. This body serves as the first responder in a highly interactive, formative, and dynamic experience. What is fundamentally clear, yet not always fully accepted or embraced, is the exquisite process of materialization itself. In our in-depth exploration of the art of 'Ulu, we find ourselves presented with a detailed template, a proposed protocol, that outlines the specific conditions surrounding our material process; these are represented by the 33 codes, which have been long held in the 33 vertebrae of the human spinal cord, each vertebra revealing itself as an intricate tool that collectively helps to construct the entirety of the human form, biologically and spiritually. Ultimately, at the culmination of the human event, at that significant moment of total materialization, do the mysterious conditions of the spiritualizing process invoke a deep and holistic transfiguration of being.

As the material is now fully accomplished, our energetic light body, often referred to as the electrical self, is finally released from its mission and can gracefully lapse into what can only be described as the enduring and profound journey along the sacred path of God. From the foundational tenet of the internal feminine, known as the ULI, we arrive at the essential criteria that affirm our sense of belonging and safety, generously radiating from the 14 vertebrae, which include the coccyx, sacral, and lumbar regions. In this process, the 'Unihipili self erupts into form itself - a true creation - with the material shaped and enhanced by various modalities, much like an artist experiencing the powerful surge of inspiration to create, to give, and to continue creating still. From the autonomy of the 'Unihipili, the codex detailing the 12 actions unfolds, while the 'Uhane vertebrae delight in the vast potential and affirming consent of the underlying infrastructure. What does the energy of God, as it flows through me, truly look, sound, taste, feel, and seem like? Transitioning from common engineering into the realm of exalted artistry, the inner masculine diligently designs the actual fashioning of our reality, capturing the power and glory inherent in the demiurge.

At the intricate bridge of the neck, seamlessly transitioning into the pronounced swell of the spherical head, the immensity of the exalted seven cervical vertebra, known as Aumākua, comes into view. This remarkable point signifies the final threshold on the profound path of materialization. It is at the opening of C7 that we encounter involution, marking the grand assessment of the self, the understanding that authenticity is indeed the only true requirement for the passage across the Hala, the transfiguration of one's being. Those of us who are unable to hear or feel the deep authority of the iwi kuamo'o risk falling prey to the mimicry of the incessant noise that distracts from beyond the obvious physical body. Intriguingly, there is no mention of reincarnation in any modern or ancient Hawaiian text, and this absence is particularly evident within the revered Mū doctrines. We can reasonably attribute this to a natural progression, a carefully selected and seamless exaltation of the material self where completion is the only outcome. It is solely when the material self is rejected, dismissed, or humiliated in its many varying forms that we distort authenticity, leading to a descent into mimicry, insecurity, escapism, and, ultimately, profound dissociation. This was not an experience shared by our ancient Mū brethren. The accomplishment of the material self, as informed by the 33 codes, was certainly not lost among the ancients, and this vital protocol remains accessible to all of us, whether we are newcomers to this material experiment or individuals who have previously explored the complex process of reincarnation. The code of C7, representing Involution, is rather telling in what must be acknowledged at the pivotal bridge leading to spiritualization—ultimately, we will indeed consume ourselves.

The total, and fully accomplished, materialization has been beautifully described as ALOHA MĀ, which embodies the concept of self-reflective love. Aloha Mā can be understood as the complete and comprehensive circumnavigation of the self, where nothing significant is left undone or untold, resulting in no feelings of dissatisfaction or regrets. The self serves as the initial vantage point, functioning as the primary reference point for all experiences. Just like our intricate journey through the spinal cord, we commence the process of navigation, moving through various codes that unveil essential tools designed to assist us on our path toward the actualization of material existence, all the while offering the promise of eventual spiritualization. At every challenge encountered, and with each initiation experienced, we come to feel the distinctive curve—a palpable and marked bend of sensational form. ALOHA can translate as "face to face," while MĀ suggests a sense of totality. The divine law of ALOHA invites us not to look away; instead, we must keep our eyes focused on the completion event, encouraging us to gather momentum as we progress through each code. Each passing vertebra contributes to the beautification of an extraordinary, incomprehensible human event, reminding us of our interconnectedness. Each code represents a bend, a curve, and as we navigate this journey, we sense that the incline is naturally leading itself back to its origin, the alpha and the omega. Perhaps a code of ALOHA, representing LOVE, is fundamentally about staying present. From this awareness, what may initially appear as something quite simple reveals itself to be a crucial aspect of this existence: we are present, self-reflective, sentient, and interactive, engaging with materials that elevate each of us to the status of alchemists and artists, capable of translating the very energy of the divine. As we find joy in the phenomenon of a diverse world of form, we come to the realization that we are simultaneously molding our most significant artifact and our greatest work of art, which is our whole self.

He inoa no mo'okū'auhau o Mahat.

ACKNOWLEDGMENTS

To my living Kumu, Bradford Ikemanu Lum, your fierce encouragement to give ALOHA and be HAWAIIAN is why I share as I do. *Mahalo piha e hoʻohui pū ʻia ko mākou mahalo mau.*

Mahalo nui to my dear friend Marni for your thoughtful edits and loving presence throughout this process. Our resilient companionship means so much to me.

And lastly, my heartfelt thanks to Sam and the team at Sam Aaron Creative for the design of this guidebook. From the vision to the final layout and launch, your clarity, creativity and guidance helped bring this project to life.

ABOUT THE AUTHOR

Ke'oni Hanalei is a Mū-Hawaiian cultural practitioner native to Maui, Hawai'i.

His fathers family derive from the highlands of Morar, Scotland and his mothers family have remained steadfast in the archipelago of *Kō Hawa'i pae 'āina* and *Papahānaumokuākea* for over 20,000 years.

His lineage is considered one of the founding families of Hawai'i.

Much of what Ke'oni shares today regarding archaic Hawaiian and Mū is rarely shared by others, and remains in moratorium by prehistoric Hawaiian families.

For Ke'oni, ALOHA is not a possession. Its only destiny is to be shared.

ALOHA MĀ.

ENTER THE PORTAL

Rarely practiced today, ʻULU is believed to be the ancestor of both Hula and Lua (Hawaiian martial arts). With only a handful of practitioners, this is a radical and heartfelt attempt to share the artistry of ʻULU with the global community.

All are welcome.

This **free introductory portal** includes recorded tutorials, instructional videos, and cultural teachings rooted in the wisdom of Mū. Your guides, Keʻoni Hanalei and Kapuahīnano Coelho, are descendants of Hawaiʻi's oldest genetic lines and are honored to share this nearly forgotten art.

Open your phone camera and scan the QR code below to join:

Prefer to type the link manually?

Visit: **ulu.pohala.net**

To explore more of Keʻoni Hanalei's work and apothecary offerings, visit: **pohala.net**

BIBLIOGRAPHY

1. Blavatsky, HP (1888a), *The Secret Doctrine*.

2. O. Nichols, C. I., Weiss, B. P., Eyster, A., Martin, C. R., Maloof, A. C., Kelly, N. M., Zawaski, M. J., Mojzsis, S. J., Watson, E. B., & Cherniak, D. J. (2024). Possible Eoarchean Records of the Geomagnetic Field Preserved in the Isua Supracrustal Belt, Southern West Greenland. *Journal of Geophysical Research: Solid Earth*, *129*(4), e2023JB027706. https://doi.org/10.1029/2023JB027706

www.ingramcontent.com/pod-product-compliance
Lightning Source LLC
Chambersburg PA
CBHW060319050426

42449CB00011B/2564